Courtesy of the author

About the Author

RUBEN "DOC" CAVAZOS is the former international president of the Mongols Motorcycle Club. He lives in California.

www.honorfewfearnone.com

Honor Few,
Fear None

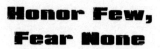

HARPER

NEW YORK · LONDON · TORONTO · SYDNEY

HONOR FEW, FEAR NONE

THE LIFE
AND TIMES
OF A MONGOL

Ruben "Doc" Cavazos

FORMER INTERNATIONAL PRESIDENT,
MONGOLS MOTORCYCLE CLUB

HARPER

Photographs courtesy of the Mongols Motorcycle Club.
The poem "Chapter 13" courtesy of Don Faris, writing as Poor Boy.

A hardcover edition of this book was published in 2008 by William Morrow, an imprint of HarperCollins Publishers.

HarperCollins books may be purchased for educational, business, or sales promotional use. For information please write: Special Markets Department, HarperCollins Publishers, 10 East 53rd Street, New York, NY 10022.

FIRST HARPER PAPERBACK PUBLISHED 2009.

Designed by Susan Walsh

Library of Congress Cataloging-in-Publication Data is available upon request.

ISBN 978-0-06-113790-7

09 10 11 12 13 OV/RRD 10 9 8 7 6 5 4 3 2 1

To my son, "Little Rubes,"
to the brothers of Chapter Thirteen,
and to the greatest fighting force on motorcycles,

the Mongols MC

CONTENTS

Author's Note   ix

1   Morning in America   1

2   Gladiator School   15

3   A Serious Man   33

4   Graduate Studies   53

5   The Greatest Motorcycle Club in the World   71

6   Old Dogs   87

7   Angels' Fall   105

8   Two Steps Forward, One Step Back   123

9   Laughlin   135

10 A Place of Our Own   153

11 A Two-Front War   169

CONTENTS

12   Something Rotten   183

13   Life Goes On   201

   Bronson: In Memoriam   207

   Epilogue   209

   Appendixes   211

   Acknowledgments   215

AUTHOR'S NOTE

My name is Ruben Cavazos. Everyone calls me Doc, so you can too. I'm fifty-one years old and the former national president—I guess now you could say former international president—of the Mongols Motorcycle Club. We've been called the most violent outlaw motorcycle gang in America and a lot of other things, most of which are B-movie fantasies. These fantasies have great power.

But the thing that's true about the Mongols is that we will not roll over and play dead. We will not turn tail. I can say proudly, both as a Mongol and as an American, that these colors don't run. We stand up. When we are attacked, we defend one another and our community, and that makes us a target from both sides of the law, and that makes for some pretty hairy times. There are things I've seen and done in my life that you may find unbelievable. I want to tell you about them and also about me. Ride with me for a while, and then make your decision.

Morning in America

About seven in the morning on May 19, 2004, I woke up to an explosion. I had just come home from my job as a radiologic technologist and slipped into sleep in my house in Pico Rivera, east of Los Angeles, when an enormous *Boom!* rattled the windows and shook the entire house. I jerked up in bed and let loose a string of curses, thinking for sure I had a gas leak in the house and something had set it off. I threw on some clothes and ran downstairs to the front door, waving to my son to stay where he was on the second floor. I didn't know if there was a fire or what. The noise seemed to come from the front, so I jerked open the front door to find out what the hell was going on.

The first thing I saw was a dozen red dots weaving around on my chest. The next thing was the string of police cars lined up along the street, diagonal to the curb, and guys crouched behind them with handguns and rifles. The red dots playing tag on my chest were the laser sights of their weapons.

I gave them the finger and slammed the door.

I might have laughed if I weren't so mad—there were a dozen police out there with heavy artillery just to take down me and my twenty-seven-year-old son? Maybe I should take it as a sign of respect, but I don't think so.

I went back to Little Rubes and told him, "We're being raided. Just sit tight and I'll see what I can do." He knows the life, so he nodded and went back into his room. Luckily my brother, Al, who also lives with us, wasn't there at the time. I picked up the phone to call one of my brother Mongols to arrange for someone to get us out of jail, since that's certainly where we would wind up. The police are after us so often that part of our club dues goes to bail and legal defense, and we always have someone we can go to for help.

But there was no dial tone. Instead, the police were on the line. They barked, "HOW MANY OF YOU ARE THERE IN THE HOUSE? COME OUT WITH YOUR HANDS UP!" I told them to fuck off and hung up. I picked it up again and they were still there, so I hung up again and tried to figure out where we stood.

I knew from experience that they probably had the house surrounded. The explosion, I found out later, had come from what they call a flash-bang grenade they'd tossed at Hooch, my dog, to let him know that he should keep out of the way. A flash-bang grenade makes a lot of noise and light but doesn't throw shrapnel. Then they would have scaled the fence until they were squeezing the house like a tourniquet. Once they were ready, they would smash the door in with a battering ram. If it came down to that, I was prepared to defend myself. Because I never know what might be coming at me, I'm always well armed.

Little Rubes came down to see what was going on, and that's when I realized I had to surrender. I didn't want anything to happen to my boy. I told him calmly that we were surrounded and that the best thing we could do would be to run with it until we could get help. "Bring some clothes," I said, "because it looks like we're going to be locked up for a while."

Now maybe they would tell me why they were attacking me. I honestly had no idea. As the head of the club, especially after all the bad publicity about us, I was under a microscope. My house was under surveillance, I was followed constantly, and my phones were tapped. I would have to be a total fool to be doing something illegal. And I wasn't—either a fool or committing any crimes. That's not why I'm in the Mongols, and that's not why the Mongols MC exists.

I picked up the phone again and told them we would be coming out. "HOW MANY OF YOU ARE IN THERE?" they said, just like a recording. I guess they were really scared that there was a gang of us ready to shoot it out with them. I hung up without answering. When Little Rubes was ready, I took him with me to the front door, pulled it open, and waited.

"PUT YOUR HANDS ON YOUR HEADS!"

We didn't say anything. I certainly wasn't going to raise my hands like the bad guy in a Roy Rogers movie. But they kept yelling, so finally I raised my hand. To give them the finger. Luckily, no one was trigger-happy, and Little Rubes and I walked out into the street.

They were mostly agents from the Bureau of Alcohol, Tobacco, Firearms and Explosives, which made me think that they were there looking for illegal weapons or drugs. That didn't worry me too much. There weren't any drugs in the house because I don't do any, and all my weapons are legal and registered. I'm not going to try to convince you that I'm Snow White. I've used drugs in my life, and I love guns. I love to shoot them, I love the way they look, and I wouldn't hesitate to use one in self-defense. But I wasn't living in a fort either. I had a nice two-story, four-bedroom house with a swimming pool and a Jacuzzi in the back. Someone had even put in lighting to show off the palm trees. It wasn't the place to hold off a siege.

The ATF agents told us we were under arrest, handcuffed us, and then took us back into the house. They made me sit on the living room couch and put Little Rubes in the kitchen for the next *nine hours,* during which time they turned the place upside down. After a while I asked one of the agents if he had a warrant. He threw it in my face. It said they had the right to search the house and confiscate any documents, weapons, bottles of pills, and so on and on. They could also take any cash or jewelry they found worth more than a thousand dollars.

What this means is this: Suppose I'm there and I've got four hundred dollars in my pocket. I've got a gold watch and some rings. Al is keeping three hundred dollars in his dresser drawer. Little Rubes has two hundred and fifty dollars and has a beautiful bracelet he was going to give to his current girlfriend. It's worth a hundred and fifty dollars. In the kitchen, we all throw our change in a huge jar, and there's sixty dollars in it. Pretty soon, the police are saying things like "We confiscated several thousand dollars worth of cash and valuables in the Cavazos residence." *All of which they keep.* As "evidence." They can figure out the crime later.

Anyway, they're tearing the house apart, looking under the carpets, flipping through every piece of paper while I'm sitting there. And sitting and sitting and sitting. I'm totally furious, yes, but I keep myself in lockdown. This kind of thing happens when you're the target of the police, as almost all Mongols are, all the time. We learn to face down the anger and adrenaline and just go with it. It's part of our lives. It's been part of my life from the time I was a child.

About the middle of the afternoon, they finally gave up after not finding anything "criminal." They had filled up boxes and boxes with my files and whatever Mongol paraphernalia I had around. One of them came over to me and said calmly, as if we were discussing the weather, "Tell us where the cash is and we'll let you off easy." I said nothing, despite the colorful response I had running through my mind. *No sense in making things worse,* I thought to myself. That's another thing you learn, not to say anything. Whatever you say, the cops will find a way to use it to keep needling you, keep wheedling and threatening and trying to make you say something more. You say nothing, you give nothing away.

After busting down every door and going through every dresser drawer, they turned up about twenty-five hundred dollars total, some of it expense money from the club, some of it mine, some of it Al's, some of it from Little Rubes. That was confiscated along with about fifteen weapons, all licensed and legal, including a shotgun, four Mini-14 rifles, four .45-caliber pistols, a couple of nines, a .30-06 hunting rifle, a .22 rifle, and one that looked like a TEC-9 (which would be illegal) but actually wasn't. I told you, I love guns.

Then one of the ATF agents said to a subordinate, "Check the cycles out." That means look at the registration numbers of the three Harleys in my garage—mine, Little Rubes's, and Al's—and check to see if any of them are listed as stolen by Motor Vehicles. One of the agents had already taken down the registration numbers and called them in, so he said, "They're clean." The first ATF agent says, looking at me, "I don't care, call Auto Theft." So two local deputies came and they went over the bikes again, and again they were clean. They took the bikes anyway. I watched as they used my own phone to call a tow truck and take my Harleys away.

Then and only then did they take us to the Pasadena police station, where the ATF had set up a base of operations. Now, I figured, we would finally find out what the fuck was going on.

I wasn't prepared for what I saw when we got there. Police cars were lined up along the whole block. Each one of them had Mongols in the back in handcuffs. There had to be thirty cars there, and since they were afraid to bring us all into the police station at one time, they were all backed up on the street. Meanwhile, all the local Pasadena cops tried to show the ATF how tough they were. They looked like kids playing cops and robbers. At one point a California Highway Patrolman, a CHP, came over to Rubes and me, leaned down, and whispered, "Great father and son team."

If that was meant to enrage me, I wasn't going to give him the satisfaction of seeing me lose it, especially in front of Little Rubes. I was really pissed, though, that my boy, whose record was completely clean, was going to have to have this on his jacket for the rest of his life. It took a little more than two more hours to get all of us booked. After that, I was moved to an interview room and told to sit at a table opposite a couple of ATF agents and two sheriff's deputies.

After a long silence, one of the Feds began to speak. "You want to talk to us, Doc?"

"About what?" I said.

"Auto theft."

Auto theft? I still had no idea what he was talking about. "I have nothing to say to you about that. Or anything." You have to be a complete idiot to tell these guys anything. Ask Martha Stewart—her lawyers tell her the same thing. Only with us, it's worse. If you tell them something, anything, they'll find a way to twist it into a story that makes you look guilty. That's exactly what was going on here.

I was put into a holding cell with several other Mongols, and that's when I found out what this was all about. We had been infiltrated by the Feds, specifically by an ATF agent named Billy Queen. We knew him as Billy St. John, and he wrote a book about being under-cover with us. I will talk more about him and his book later on, but this raid was the result of his two years of spying on us. He had spent that time asking every Mongol he met whether he could get him drugs or illegal weapons and where our motorcycles came from. The police were trying to prove that we were stealing motorcycles and then fixing them up so that they wouldn't be recognized. They were trying to accuse the Mongols of some sort of conspiracy to commit auto theft on a nationwide basis. At that time, very few motorcycle parts had identification numbers, so they were very hard to trace and the cops needed a way to know when something was stolen.

Since we don't do that, at least not as a club, they eventually had to resort to trying to trick us into committing crimes. That's what they had on me. I had been supplementing my income for a while by working with a chrome factory and shop in Santa Ana. Chroming is very important when you're customizing a Harley. Chrome becomes a statement all its own. As with porcelain figurines or a classic car, the excellence is in the detail. You start doing parts of your bike that don't come chromed from the factory, and when you put it all back together something stands out about that bike. I was doing a lot of that when I was rebuilding one of my bikes, taking everything to a friend who owned the chrome shop in Santa Ana.

My friend's business was a little slow, so he offered me a deal. He knew that I was the head of the Mongols Motorcycle Club, and he said that if I would bring jobs to him, he would give me half of the money he made. He would do the work at a big discount, to keep the cost to the brothers down. I told him he didn't have to give me anything as long as he passed the discount along to the brothers. He said that was great and that he'd do chroming for me for free. It sounded like a pretty good deal—for me, for him, and for my brothers. I began to encourage Mongols to send their business to him, through me. Everybody was happy.

I began making regular trips back and forth from my house to his shop, taking and picking up various chrome parts. One day Billy Queen came by and dropped off a front fork he needed chromed. I wasn't home at the time, so Little Rubes took care of him. Rubes put the piece into the corner of the hallway where I stack all the parts for my next run to the shop. A few weeks later, when the piece was finished, I returned it to Billy. He paid for the job, thanked me for the favor, and that, I thought, was that.

In fact, Billy had brought over the front end of a motorcycle that the cops knew was stolen. According to the police, because I took it over to the chrome shop, I was dealing in stolen goods. It was as if I was running an auto repair shop and you brought a Volkswagen in and asked me to fix the transmission. I do my job, you take the car away, and then you put on your badge and come back and arrest me because the car is stolen. When you take your car in, do you think the garage runs the number through the DMV to see if it was stolen? Did I check with my brother Mongols and ask them, "Is this part stolen? Is that part stolen?" No, I didn't, and you can imagine how they would have reacted if I had. So if I had said to those ATF agents that I didn't deal in any stolen parts, which was the truth as far as I knew, they would have been able to call me a liar in court. If the Feds played their cards right, they could blow the story up into a large-scale motorcycle theft operation.

Late that afternoon they loaded me and about a dozen other Mongols, including Rubes, into a van for the trip down to the county jail. There we were booked and put into separate cells until one of our boys on the outside called the bail bondsman that the Mongols had on constant retainer just for bullshit like this. Once I was out, I made some calls and found that Little Rubes wasn't given bail! This was totally insane. Only murderers and child molesters don't make bail. I called John Ciccone, one of the Feds whose name I'd been given during the interrogation. (If you read Billy Queen's book, you know that Ciccone was the one who had started Queen's undercover operation.)

"This is Doc," I said to him. "Do you know who I am?"

"I know you," he said. "What's up, Ruben?"

"You know what's up," I said. "You guys made a big mistake. Why are you keeping my son in without bail?"

A long silence followed. When Ciccone finally spoke, he sounded like a guy at a poker table who had drawn four aces. "You want me to help him, Ruben?"

"You know I do."

"Are you going to talk to us?"

So that was it. They must have wanted me to name some names. They could make the whole thing go away if I cooperated with them. I said no way. "I told you before. I'm not talking to you guys. That's final."

"Are you sure, Ruben?"

"You know me. What in my past would make you think that I would turn somebody in? After all I've been through, what makes you think I would change now?" More silence. "Now you talk to me and tell me why you have Rubes when you know the charges against him won't stick."

I could hear Ciccone put the phone down heavily on his desk. After several minutes he came back. "You're right," he said. "It's a mistake."

"Fix it."

"I will."

"How soon?"

He hung up. There was nothing I could do now but wait. I went back home, and a full twenty-four hours after he was arrested, we were able to bail out Little Rubes and he was released.

A couple of months later, we all had to appear before a grand jury to answer questions to see if they could indict us under the RICO Act. My response was no response. I pled the Fifth Amendment, as my lawyer instructed me to. When I was finally allowed to step down I walked directly out of the courtroom. They had nothing on him, or me, and the charges didn't stick.

It was from there that my brothers and I started talking with one another about what had happened and what it felt like to beat the case. Out of pure pride at being Mongols, we all hit the street at one time. We wanted to show the world that we were still free. We showed up at our usual places, and people looked at us and said, "What are you doing here? We thought you were locked up." We rode in groups of ten, sometimes more, sometimes whole chapters, showing off our colors all around Pasadena, as far down as San Diego and into the Central Valley as well. Any Mongol whose patches had been confiscated in the raid (and there were many) wore his insignia T-shirt. Those whose bikes were still being held by the Feds rode along in cars. We hit all our regular spots, the clubs, the bars, and partied all night long. I hung mostly in Pico, where I was greeted with hugs and applause from my boys and free drinks from the bar owners.

Hey, look, I know that not everyone in the Mongols is a saint. If I tried to pass that off as the truth, I'd be as bad as the cops. But they want the public to think that every Mongol is a brutal, ruthless criminal and a drug addict. There are some good cops, I'll say it right here. The problem is, it's usually the bad ones who come after us.

Like any American citizen, a Mongol has the right to defend himself. A Wall Streeter or a Wilshire Boulevard executive defends himself—not the way we do, but in ways that can be equally destructive to you and me. Sure, there's a certain amount of machismo associated with a Mongol, but if that isn't machismo on Wall Street, I don't know what is. Our worlds are very different, in many ways, but respect is basic to both of them. If a businessman loses the respect of the people he works with, he won't get ahead. He may even lose his job. But his world offers support and opportunities that don't exist in East L.A.

If a Mongol loses the respect of the people around him, he might as well be dead. And in my world, if you let the law tell you how to live your life and what to do, you lose respect. That's true whether you're a Mongol or not. So we stand up to the law, and that makes us a target; that forces us to defend ourselves and demand respect while doing it. That sets us apart from the average guy walking down the street, and that's exactly what the police and the Feds can't stand.

The grand jury never returned an indictment, but that didn't stop the ATF. After a few months, the case came back to life, but this time we were all charged with receiving stolen property. You see, the Feds put so much time and money into these undercover operations, they want to be able to show some results. I mean, an FBI agent told us they had been developing this case for about three years. Billy had been hanging around the Mongols for about a year, wearing a wire to record conversations. Anyway, at this trial Billy went on and on about the stolen motorcycles he had delivered to that shop I worked with, playing the recordings he made while wearing the wire and trying to make a case.

He testified that when he dropped off that front fork at the house, he'd told Little Rubes that the part was from a stolen bike and that Rubes had said okay, no problem. He also testified that he'd informed us that it was a stolen part. We asked him to prove that he'd said that, to let us hear the recording from the wire he was wearing. Unfortunately for the Feds, fortunately for me, Billy's wire somehow "wasn't working" the day we had our "discussion" about the fork. Of course there were no witnesses to that conversation or to his conversation with Rubes. The courts didn't think too much of that, evidently. Eventually all charges against Little Rubes, me, and most of the Mongols caught in the roundup were dropped.

I thought that was finally the end of it until a few months later, when I received a letter ordering me to report to superior court in Whittier to answer a charge of possession of an illegal firearm. I knew right then that I was again guilty until proven innocent. They had to be talking about one of the guns the Feds had confiscated during the raid, so I took all the information about the guns down to the nearest gun shop and checked them out. They were all legal, even the one that looked like a TEC-9. It had none of the operational features that would make it illegal. Then I learned that the guns they listed as being the ones they took from my house weren't the guns they took at all! They had put down the names of different guns, guns that were indeed illegal.

I showed up for court in Whittier, but I also went over to the district attorney's office and found out which deputy district attorney the case had been assigned to. I just wanted to speak plainly and openly and try to short-circuit this whole mess. I found her standing in the hallway and walked up to her, something prosecutors do not like. I'm a big man, and of course many people believe the tall tales that are told about Mongols. Obviously I had no intention of doing anything to her other than to speak as one human being to another. I tried to explain that this was all a big mistake, that the weapons were all legal.

Before I was able to get very far with my explanation, she held up her hand as if she were stopping traffic and informed me in a strong but even voice that it was inappropriate for me to talk with her outside the courtroom. Then she turned and walked away, like she had no time for me. I started to get mad and said, "Are you interested in justice or are you just interested in hanging me? Check out those guns they're holding. They're not the ones on the indictment."

Later, in the courtroom, she got up before the judge and asked for a slight delay. The judge asked why, and she explained that she was waiting for confirmation via telephone from the LAPD's weapons expert as to the validity of the charge. I was thinking that either the deputies were idiots or they were trying to frame me. When we reconvened, she approached the bench and in a voice that could barely be heard, she said that the weapons were in fact legal. At that, the judge dismissed all charges against me. Before the judge could leave the bench, I was on my feet. "Your Honor," I said, "I'd like my weapons back."

He didn't have a chance to answer at first, because one of the arresting deputies stood up and said that further tests were needed to make sure that none of the guns had been converted to an automatic weapon—even though they had had the weapons in their possession for months. "OK," the judge said, "but if they are legal, return them to Mr. Cavazos as soon as you're done." With that, the judge disappeared into his chambers.

My weapons were never returned.

It would take three full years for me to be able to pick up my bikes. I had to keep calling and filling out forms and then calling some more and filling out some more forms. When I finally had all the paperwork ready to go and was walking into the courtroom to claim my property, they stopped me in the hallway and said they were going to return my bike, but not Little Rubes's or my brother's. I figured that I would fight those battles another day, so I left the court and called my son to get a tow truck down to the impound lot where the bikes were being kept.

But when I got to the impound lot myself, an ATF agent suddenly popped out from behind a corner, and six screaming black-

and-whites pulled up behind me. The ATF agent informed me that I was being charged with auto theft—*again*—and clapped me into a Whittier jail. It was the same charge, the same case, but they had been able to transfer it to a different court—just to see if they could get a better result.

Little Rubes was also rearrested, and once again we were interrogated, said nothing, and made bail. The case was no better than it was before, and by the time the charges were brought to superior court, this time in the city of El Monte, they were tossed by the judge. Billy Queen was there too, standing off to one side surrounded by security guards. I approached him, and the security tensed. I said to him, "You miss riding with us, don't you?"

He said, "Yeah, I do."

This second case was just their way of making my life miserable. I think they knew the case would be thrown out, but this way, they could arrest me and Little Rubes twice, make us pay bail twice, and make us pay the lawyers twice.

You see, they aren't really interested in justice, except maybe for that one deputy DA. They want to succeed in their jobs; they want to get promoted. If they don't like you, they will make your life hell. The Feds were and still are trying to put me away for life. How do I know this? *Because they told me so.* More than once they've said, "We're going to get you for everything you and your guys do." If that were really true, my life would be a picnic. Most Mongols never commit a crime. But the Feds are trying to imprison me for things that I don't do. I don't know if you can call it entrapment or what, but that is justice for me and my brother Mongols and for many other people in this world. How can I respect that?

I have learned the first rule of living my life the hard way. That's why the tattoo on my chest reads "Respect few, fear none."

2

Gladiator School

One of the few people I respect was my father, though, without meaning to, he put me in the middle of the gladiator school that was East Los Angeles. He was Alvaro Cavazos, and he came to the United States from Mexico to find work. I was born on December 28, 1956, at Cook County Hospital, Chicago. My mother was Linda Romo, but they parted when I was two years old. That's all I ever found out about her. I'm not sure if they ever married formally, but they had two sons, me and Alvaro Jr., who was three years older. In the few pictures I have, my mother looks very midwestern in a dress, a pearl necklace, and high heels. As the daughter of German/Irish/Spanish immigrants who lived in southern Texas, she was probably raised very much according to the rules of the time. Taking up with my father might have been the most daring thing she had ever done. I can remember seeing her only four times. I think she's still alive and lives somewhere in Texas, but other than that I haven't got a clue.

Maybe I was born in Chicago because it was winter and my father could not earn any money picking on the farms or collecting trash, which he also did. Early on, my parents decided to move to Texas, near the Mexican border, where my mother still had relatives who could help out, I guess. My father's Mexican-Spanish parents, also immigrants, lived just across the border in Nuevo Laredo, Mexico, so that was a reason to go there too. In those days crossing the border was no big deal. Laredo, Texas, and Nuevo Laredo, Mexico, were really one city, so people crossed the border every day, sometimes many times a day. Nobody searched you.

In Texas, we lived mostly among farmworkers and ranchers. My father worked the fields, one of those Tex-Mex field hands who wear the hat and boots, like a cowboy. Sometime around my fifth birthday, my dad couldn't find decent work in Texas or Nuevo Laredo or anywhere else nearby. One day he threw me and my older brother into the backseat of his beat-up old Buick sedan and drove us all out west to start new lives in Los Angeles. Very new lives.

I remember that ride well. The car chugged along the road like a coffee percolator on a hot stove while I was stuck in the big backseat, which was as comfortable as a park bench. No one had ever heard of air-conditioning, so we were used to the heat, but it was not fun. At night we'd all sleep stretched out on picnic tables, probably in a park or at a rest stop.

My dad kept big gallon containers of water in the car for whenever the radiator overheated, which was always. The engine also leaked oil by the gallon, so he would have to make frequent stops at gas stations and ask whoever was there if they had any used oil he might have for free. He kept whatever they gave him in the back of the car, next to the plastic gallons of water. It made the whole car stink. I remember thinking that this trip was taking forever because we had to keep stopping to refill the oil and let the engine cool off. My father was like that Buick, pointed in the right direction but unable to get very far without working hard all the time.

I hated that backseat. Backseats are for two types of people—rich guys and prisoners. I remember at one point a big, noisy bike passed us on the left, fast like a rocket. Now that was the way to go, I told myself.

On the blistering day we crossed Arizona, something blew under the hood, and the Buick came to a lurching, wheezing stop somewhere between Phoenix and the California border. After a while a friendly Hispanic guy came by in a tow truck. He pulled over and took a look to see if he could figure out what was wrong. "Something's broken underneath," he said. My dad told him he didn't have enough money to fix it, but the guy towed us anyway. He took us to an old garage not too far away that looked like an airplane hangar. He said he would weld the crack for free but warned my dad that it wouldn't hold very long. "You might make it all the way to California," he said, "but then you got to either fix it right or dump the thing."

The job took longer than the man thought, and by nightfall it still wasn't done. That night we all slept inside the car, locked in the garage. In the morning the man returned and finished the job. When my dad thanked him and again said he had no money, the guy shrugged his shoulders, wished him well, and we were on our way. That meant something to me. It taught me a lesson about being part of some brotherhood that takes care of its own.

Of course when you limp into California in a half-dead Buick, you don't have your choice of where you're going to live. My dad didn't go to a real estate agent and look over properties. We went to family. For a while we lived in the back of a tiny garage my dad rented from a cousin who lived in Cypress Park, a Mexican ghetto in L.A., which in those days consisted mostly of dirt roads, junkyards, and liquor stores. At night I could hear guns going off so often I thought they were fireworks.

My dad was a hard worker and always held down two or three jobs at a time. At the beginning he worked in two different gas stations, but something must have happened, because I remember being at the unemployment office with him not long after we arrived. He was looking for work, but he had to bring me and Al because there was no one else to take care of us. Then a flatbed truck pulled up in front of us. It came from the new South Central General Motors plant, which had just opened and needed people to work. Dad pulled Al and me onto the truck, and we went over there and he filled out the application and got a job that day. He worked there for the rest of his life, starting out as a janitor working nights.

During the day he pumped gas at a station on Avenue 26, not far from our house. One time when I was a kid I remember asking him if I could get a job at the General Motors plant someday. "Son," he said, "I'd love you to, but you'd go to jail for murder the first month if you had to work among these black guys who hate us. Let me tell you, every night when it's time to punch out, they push to the front of the line ahead of us. They call us spics." I'd never heard that word before, but I knew what he meant. He knew that I was something of a hothead and that I wouldn't tolerate being pushed around or bullied. He wanted to warn me away from that. He loved me and I loved him. Ironically, twenty-five years later my closest coworker would be a black man, Ted Nichols.

I attended Loreto Elementary School on Arroyo Seco Avenue. My very first day there, a kid came up to me with a big smile, stuck out his hand, and said, "My name is Filemon and I am the toughest kid in school, so you and I have to go a few rounds to make sure I'm right." He didn't tell me where or when, but I knew that one day we were going to have to go at it. He was a good-size kid, with big shoulders and ham fists. I was already tall for my age but still very skinny and wasn't sure I could take him. I wasn't used to the violence, but I wasn't scared of it either.

But boxing wasn't the only difference between East Los Angeles and Texas. I remember one kid in elementary school who just fell over in the schoolyard one day and downers, or "reds," spilled out of his pocket. We knew nothing of this kind of life before we crossed the desert to Los Angeles. We were just regular kids.

One day after school, Filemon was waiting for me on the street, and we went at it. I took a few lumps, but I held my own. For the next two weeks, there was one fight after another, but I didn't start them, the other kids did. I had a temper, but I wasn't a bully. It was either fight when you were challenged or lose respect. Respect was very important to me. It was to all of us. We didn't have much, but we were determined to have respect. In that world, if you stand up for yourself and fight, people will respect you. If you don't, then you get your ass kicked anyway. Los Angeles was gladiator school.

By the time I was in maybe fourth grade, we got out of the apartment we had been living in and moved up the hill to Ulysses Street, which was kind of a famous street at the time—for its gangs. It was very steep, and we were near the top. It looks like a quiet Los Angeles street, with those little California bungalows with maybe a postage stamp piece of grass in the front yard. The houses were right next to one another, packed along the narrow street. Ours was a little different because it had a half basement and was a wood-frame house. It had two bedrooms and a porch in the back—nothing special, but not a pit. The bathroom was off the back porch, and on winter mornings, it was cold, colder than Texas. When it got really cold, we would leave the stove on for heat. That was all we could do.

I would wake up in the morning, and if there was something to eat, I ate. If there wasn't, I didn't. Sometimes my father was there and sometimes he was working. Al and I were basically on our own. In fact, the police were always coming around because we were too young to be left alone, but there was nothing my father could do about it.

My best friend at the time was a guy named Robert Medley, or Huero, as everyone called him because of his fair skin. He was big, blond, and blue-eyed, but if you weren't looking at him, just heard him talking, you would swear he was Hispanic. His mother was Hispanic, and his father was a big friendly redneck who drove Caterpillar tractors and had a heart as big as a house. I met Huero almost as soon as we moved to the neighborhood. He'd grown up among tough kids and had learned how to handle himself.

Physically, I had this nervous tic that went through my body like a wave of electricity. It always started in my stomach and rose up through my shoulders, where I could shake it out of my body. It made me look like one of those bad guys in the movies who moved funny, like Humphrey Bogart or James Cagney. It also made me look tougher than I already was, like there was an energy in me wanting to break out and you better not be in the way.

Even with all the fighting, there weren't really gangs in elementary school. You could still be something like a normal kid. I sold newspapers on the corner and played ball in the street. At that time, Hispanics had very large families; six kids was not unusual, and at least one family had twelve. So on a summer night, there could be thirty or forty kids out on the street at any given time, and the parents weren't usually keeping an eye on us. They were working or exhausted from working. There was a lot of poverty around me. I would walk into a home and find mattresses on the floor where my friends slept and the refrigerator wouldn't be working anymore—but that didn't matter, because there was no food in it anyway—and the toilet didn't work. They would have to go to the gas station on the corner to take a crap.

Later, in junior high school, the gangs came into your life. I was in Florence Nightingale Junior High, and there were gangs of kids that would control the school. They would walk in a group down the center of the hall and take up all the room, so that people would have to lean up against their lockers to let them by. There were drinking fountains that only they could use. There were fights all the time, and eventually you just wound up in a gang because even if you didn't want to take all that crap, you couldn't fight them all. You could take maybe two or three of them, but there would always be more coming. Even with Huero to back me up, there were always more coming.

Huero and I were inseparable. We liked to hang out on the street corner or, if we needed privacy, inside the long, dark flood-control tunnels that ran along the freeways. Huero and I got into reds and sniffing glue, the kind used to make those plastic model airplanes. Not heroin, though it was a popular drug at the time. But what we really liked was girls.

I was fourteen the first time I had sex. There were these two pretty girls who lived right by us. They were fifteen years old, but they were very well developed, so they seemed like thirty to me. One day I took one of them to an abandoned house down the street from where I lived. There was an old mattress in one of the rooms. We started fooling around on it, and next thing I knew I was fucking her but good. She loved it almost as much as I did.

Later on that night I happened to run into Huero, who had a crush on a girl named Maria. I told him what I'd done in the abandoned house, and he got this crazy look on his face. Then he said he wanted to watch me have sex with my girl. So the next time I was going to take her there, I tipped off Huero, and he hid in the room next door and watched us through a broken heater vent. I told him to be sure not to make any noise, but he got so excited he couldn't help it and he started jerking off.

"What was that?" the girl yelped.

"Nothing," I said and kept right on.

Afterward, I asked Huero if he wanted me to fix him up with my girl's sixteen-year-old sister. I told him she was nice, much nicer than Maria, but he was true to his dream, so he said no. I set him up anyway, for his own good. We went on a double date, and after a movie all four of us went back to the abandoned house and fucked. A few nights later we did it again, only this time we switched girls. After that, Maria was history.

My older brother wasn't interested in gangs; he was more of a loner. But Alvaro could handle himself if he needed to, he could fight. Everyone did. Everyone had to, otherwise they'd be dead. He could shoot the streetlights out with a snub-nosed .38, and he often did. He had very good aim. He always dressed well. His friends used to call him "Al the Suit." I was never sure if they were praising him or making fun of him, but that was his problem.

I didn't join a gang officially until I was eleven or twelve. I went to some kind of local festival in Highland Park, and I got into an argument with someone who was in the Cypress Park gang. We started to box, and I was doing pretty well until the rest of the gang jumped me. I got a bloody nose and a fat lip, some bruises. It wasn't really a big deal. In those days you fought so much that taking a beating wasn't all that unusual, so I just walked home. Before I got there a lowrider pulled up with four members of a different gang, the Avenues. They knew me from the neighborhood and asked me what had happened. I told them and they asked, "Do you want to have a fair fight with the one guy who started the whole thing?"

"Hell yes."

"Well, we can help you with this problem, but you have to become one of us." That was OK with me. I didn't realize then what I was getting into, that, after this, violence would become a regular part of my life.

They told me to go home, get cleaned up. The next day they showed up and we drove to an alley where the other gang hung out. I called the one guy out, and soon I had him on his back and was beating the shit out of him. Next thing I knew the other Cypress Gang members were beating me—*again*. So naturally the Avenues, who were a much tougher, more hard-core gang, joined in. It didn't stop until the police screeched up to the alley.

Becoming an Avenue meant I would have to be initiated, which meant being beaten up by a bunch of them. I guess the idea was that if you could stand being beaten up by them, you wouldn't cave in when other gangs beat up on you. At least I didn't have to go through it alone. Huero wanted to join the Avenues as well. The process was simple and brutal. We were called to the back of a house in Highland Park where six or seven members of the Avenues were waiting for us. They asked us if we wanted to drink a few beers first or just get it over with. My first thought was I didn't want to throw up over all of them, so I said, Let's go. They gathered around us in a circle, and the next thing we knew we were getting punched all over. It was not enough just to put our hands up and take it. We had to fight back, to show that we could give as well as get. When it was all over, Huero and I were members of the Avenues and proud of it.

From then on, my life was the Avenues. We would meet before school in the morning and decide which classes we would go to. You might say, "I want to go to my second-period class and my third-period class," because maybe you liked the subject, or there was a girl you liked to see, or maybe you were actually doing well in that class.

But it was a mark of a gangbanger that you never carried books. You carried a folder—it was supposed to have your work in it, but ours just had graffiti all over. It wasn't simply that we hated school, or that the school didn't care what we did. There were some teachers who really cared. Some just wanted to harass you, but others would sit you down and warn you that you would have a hard life if you didn't turn it around right now. There were vice principals who would drive around the neighborhoods in their own cars looking for kids, to try to help them.

But the kids in that neighborhood—all the neighborhoods around—they couldn't see themselves in the future. They didn't see anything beyond their street, their neighborhood. All they cared about was having respect in their neighborhood. I was the same way. I wanted the respect of the kids around me, and that meant being a gangbanger.

Once I was in, the Avenues gave me my first real sense of belonging to something. I felt good about being with people my own age who cared about me, who protected me, who understood what I was all about. When my dad didn't have enough money to buy me shoes, they got them to me (I'm not saying they bought them). Or if one of us was hungry, we'd share whatever food we had, down to the last tortilla. I never felt like I was taking anything away from anybody and, more important, I never felt out of place among my own. I also got the hottest girls in the neighborhood.

I started dressing the part. Khakis replaced my jeans, and they had to be creased all the way down. A muscle shirt instead of a ripped tee, a dress shirt or sweater folded perfectly over my arm. We started wearing Hush Puppies instead of sneakers.

I think a lot of people believe that the neighborhood gangs sit around plotting crimes, like they're some kind of junior Mafia. Law enforcement encourages that idea because gangs are an easy target, so you always hear that the gangs are trafficking in drugs or guns or maybe extortion. All these things can happen, but that isn't really the way it works, at least not when I was in a gang.

Not that we didn't commit crimes, but we had been doing that all along. Small things like writing graffiti or shoplifting, but also stealing cars or holding up fast-food joints. When I was very small, there was a distribution center for Hostess bakery goods not too far away, and at night these big semis would deliver the day's stock. The driver would park and open the gate, and as he walked back to the cab of the truck, we would run inside the compound and hide behind a Dumpster. While he was unloading we would be in the back of the truck, eating away. We were just small children, but where do you draw the line?

Stealing was just another way of surviving. We didn't have any money, and sometimes we didn't have any food. I mean, I was very happy with rice and beans, and I could live on a tortilla with salt, and there were times when I ate a ketchup sandwich for dinner. But if there was nothing, I would put my gun in the waistband of my pants, put a shirt over it, and go down to the Jack in the Box.

Of course it wasn't always that restaurant, but I had a particular thing for Jack in the Box for some reason. I would go in and order a ton of food. This was when you paid only after you got the food. Now they make you pay first, because of guys like me. So the person at the counter—let's say it's a guy—would bring the food and put it on the counter. Then I'd say, "Oh, and I'd like a large Coke," and while he turned around to get the Coke, I would pull out my gun so that when he came back, I would have the gun pointed at his nose. "Oh, and while you're at it," I'd say, "give me all the money in the register." And I would walk away with my hamburgers and a hundred dollars.

One time I was going back to hold up a Jack in the Box that

I'd held up before, and I decided I needed a disguise. So I went to the drugstore and shoplifted some cotton pads and medical tape and taped them on both sides of my nose, as if it were broken. When I walked into the Jack in the Box, it was about two in the morning, but there were a couple of guys there waiting for their food. They looked at me and started laughing and making jokes. I thought, *What assholes, making fun of a poor guy who's had an accident.* And I'm thinking, *I hate bullies.* So the food comes and I do my routine about the Coke and pull out the gun. Their faces just went white— like *Oh my god, we fucked up bad.* I turned and pointed the gun at them and I said, "What's so funny now, assholes?" It was a small moment of satisfaction. There weren't many.

By the way, I didn't get any money this time because the employees panicked and hit the floor and wouldn't get up to open the register. I couldn't get them to get up. I asked them in English and Spanish and they still wouldn't get up. But I wasn't going to hurt them, so all I got was the burgers and a little satisfaction.

Even while I was still in junior high school I hung out with guys who were always trying different drugs. We used to cut classes, get high, and drive around looking for clothes hanging out to dry on clotheslines. We'd jump the fence and grab all the clean socks. Then we'd go into a hardware store and buy or steal a can of clear plastic lacquer or ignition spray, anything that had a flammable chemical in it. We'd spray one side of the sock until it was soaking wet, roll it up onto itself, then put it in our mouths and breathe deeply through the material. The chemicals would go straight to our brains and make us crazy.

I stole my first car because I wanted the wheels, not the car. I went downtown to Chinatown, where there was a festival going on. Festivals are very convenient places to steal cars. Many people have to park pretty far away from the festival, and they're going to enjoy themselves there, so the car is going to be parked for a while. You can just sit and watch until a car comes along that you want. Sure enough, there was this beautiful white '58 Chevy that had the perfect rims. In those days, the old ignition systems were very simple, with one-sided keys, and Chevy only made about thirty different keys. The Avenues had a ring with all the different kinds of keys, and one of them would start a Chevy, guaranteed.

So I took this car that night and I drove it to my old grammar school to take the wheels off. You're always on the lookout for the cops, so you start by loosening the lugs. If there's still no one around, you jack up the car and take the tires and wheels off. But just when I was ready to jack the car up, a police prowl car drove by. I jumped in the Chevy and took off. I had almost made it home when all of a sudden the front wheels popped off. I felt and heard a huge crash, and I saw the wheels rolling off down the street, going every which way. All the neighbors came out to see about the noise, and I'm sitting there in a car with no wheels on it. I jumped out of the car and started to take off, but then I realized my fingerprints were all over the car, so I found an old T-shirt in the back and wiped the seats and the steering wheel and the rest. Everyone gradually just went back into their houses while I worked on that, and when I was finished, I walked home.

Basically our crew only had one car at a time. When we first started stealing cars we didn't have licenses because we were too young, but someone always had a car. If you were the one who had the car, you were the man, but your car was everybody's car. We would drive my old '62 Impala until we ran out of gas. We would push it to a gas station, and everyone would bring out a few dollars to fill it up. You would drive it for a week or two like it was your car—you washed it, cleaned it, changed the oil, kept it running. Then after a while you realized it was time to get a different one, if you hadn't already wrecked the first, so you ditched that car and stole another one. Usually we stole cars from someplace far away, since we didn't want to steal a neighbor's car.

By the time I was fourteen, I had accomplished a lot, in the terms a gangbanger would appreciate. Like getting arrested. I say fourteen, but you know, maybe it was thirteen or fifteen and maybe I was at this school or that school. It all blends into the same thing, the same time, the same people. We all knew that we were going to be arrested sometime for something, so our attitude was *OK, I might as well get it over with.* The first time I was ever busted for anything was for sniffing glue, but I was arrested as a juvenile, so I went to juvenile court and wound up in juvenile hall. If you were young and got arrested they'd take you there until you got to court, maybe for a week or ten days. I was there like one day. I didn't consider that a serious arrest.

It always seemed to me that juvenile hall was more about trying to scare you than about trying to punish or change you. They tried to make it look more like a school—there were dorms and classes, but there was also barbed wire on the fences. You met some hard-core kids in there, some runaways, and some kids who should not have been there at all because they weren't really troublemakers. They were the ones who had been blamed for somebody else's deal or were just along for the ride when things went bad. Or they had just done a little dope. The new law for drug offenses is that you get treatment instead of confinement, and that's good, because a lot of kids who weren't really gangbangers when they went in were turned into gangbangers by the time they got out. I went in as one of the hard-core kids.

A few of the Avenues were always in juvenile hall, so I had friends, and actually you tried to get along with all the kids from other gangs as long as you were locked up. There wasn't really a gang thing in juvenile hall. If you saw one of your rivals there, you just ignored him, and vice versa. I guess that's a necessity. Otherwise we would have been trying to kill one another all the time. Can you imagine what a nightmare that would be? No way would the staff have been able to stop us.

The staff were not like guards you have in a prison. These people were more like social workers. They would try to find out why you were in a gang or doing drugs or stealing, but most of us had the attitude *This is me; this is what I do; don't try to change me.* If I remember correctly they would ask something like, "Why did you hold up that 7-Eleven?" I would shrug my shoulders. There wasn't much conversation with them; I just shrugged my shoulders a lot. I wasn't a very talkative person; at the most I would just say, "I needed money." They would ask, "Why did you steal the car?" And I would say I needed to get from point A to point B.

Juvenile hall is right behind County Medical, where I work now. From the top windows of the hospital I can see into the yard. We have patients from there; the staff bring the kids over and we X-ray them or CT-scan them. If I asked them what they were in for, they would probably just shrug their shoulders.

The first time I ever spent time in a jail happened because I was in a car with a couple of the Avenues when the driver, who was high on the cheap wine we generally drank, got lost and made a U-turn across a double white line into a parking lot. Unfortunately, it was the parking lot of the local police station, and they weren't amused. A couple of them came over to find out what was going on. Next thing we knew, we were spending the night in a cell. That was my introduction to sleeping on a slab mattress, my first night behind bars. I wasn't afraid; in fact, I was proud. I thought I had passed another test and that it was a good thing.

My first serious arrest was when Huero and I and a few of the other guys tried to rob a convenience store. I didn't know we were going to do this, I thought we were just going to steal some liquor. The store was crowded, but I went to the back and shoved a couple of bottles of cheap wine into my waistband and covered them with my jacket. What I didn't know was that one of the boneheads I was with had a gun and had decided to rob the register while we were there. I was turning around to walk out when I saw this guy holding up the register. I was surprised but I thought, *What the hell. It's part of the program.*

The guy who was driving the car was not a member of the Avenues, but he hung around with us and they got the number of his license plate and arrested him. He ratted everybody out, and the next morning around 5:00 A.M. the police raided my home and arrested me for armed robbery. We were locked up for a couple months at juvenile hall and then we were put on probation.

I wasn't the only one stealing or doing drugs, by any stretch of the imagination. East L.A. was like the Wild West or the jungle. Anything could happen, anything. I remember walking along the street one day when an old lady staggered by me with a huge bullet hole in her chest. I guess her husband had shot her. We helped her and called an ambulance. That kind of thing was just part of your life. I remember her, so it's not like women were always wandering the streets with bullet holes in them, but shootings were very common. You didn't stop to think that it should be different, or that it was wrong, or that you should live somewhere else. You couldn't live anywhere else, but you also didn't really know anyplace different. That's not saying it doesn't affect you, but it affects different people in different ways. Some people crack; some get stronger. I got stronger.

When it was finally time for me to graduate from junior high school, I needed some new clothes for the ceremony so I went to the May department store in downtown L.A. I was wearing baggy pants and gathered up all the clothes I wanted, put them on under my own clothes, and walked out. I had everything I needed except shoes. For shoes, I had to go to a store downtown, a Florsheim on Broadway. They had tables with the shoes displayed outside, but only one shoe from each pair so they wouldn't be stolen. I took one. Then I went down the street to another Florsheim and took another, same style.

Then I realized I had taken two left shoes. That didn't stop me. I just took one of the shoes back to the first store and told them they'd given me two left shoes. They were very surprised, but they exchanged it right away. At my junior high school graduation, every piece of clothing I had on, from my underwear to my tie, was stolen. It's amazing what you can do when you have the nerve.

3

A Serious Man

The gangs were my secondary education in gladiator school. In addition to giving you that sense of identity, of having allies, of brotherhood, they also gave you enemies. There was always a history with the gang, old scores to settle—maybe some so old that no one knew when they started. Others happened last week. Another gang killed a member of your gang, so that score had to be settled. You killed one of theirs, and so on and so on.

It wasn't that anyone ordered a hit. No one told you to do something. The gangs didn't have presidents who issued orders anyway. There were the *veteranos,* the ones who had survived the longest, and there were others who had status for other reasons—because they stood up and handled business, whether it was fighting anyone who challenged you or if it was doing a drive-by. What would happen is that a bunch of the gang members would be sitting around on the porch, having a few beers, and you would talk about a person you'd lost. Very sad. Eventually one person might nod to another and say, "All right, let's do it." And he would go to the trunk of his car and pull out a rifle, throw it in the front seat, and they would drive off.

I was maybe thirteen or fourteen the first time that a friend sitting on my porch was hit by a gunshot. He was not the last either—my house was shot up several times. It was part of being a gangbanger. Since we were on such a steep and narrow street, rival gangs didn't necessarily drive by us. They would stop at the intersection down the hill and just shoot upward. Or downward, from the hills that rose up above our house. There was one particular house, on a hill maybe two hundred yards from our place, and I guess they knew somebody there, because they would shoot at us from that house. This was before the gangs agreed not to shoot into houses, in order to avoid shooting mothers and kids.

I did it too. You would go out looking for the guy who was responsible. If you couldn't find him, you might go by his house and shoot it up. I remember one time the plan was that my buddy would hide across the street with his rifle while I went up to the front door and knocked. I'd step aside, and when our target came to the door, my buddy would shoot. But our target's life was saved when his mother answered the door instead.

If I drive down my street today and look at the houses, it would take me more than two hands to count the dead and wounded. My buddy across the street, Richard Lewis, was shot and killed just a few streets away. In the next house, across from me, the guy was stabbed and almost died. Next door to me, a friend of the family was stabbed and killed. Stephen Baca. I looked up to him; I thought he was the coolest gangster I'd ever seen. Two doors down, stabbed. Across the street, shot but survived. Two houses down from that, this guy was shot or stabbed thirteen times before the one that killed him. He was a guy who grew up in the neighborhood. And at the intersection near my house was where little Jojo lived. He was shot and killed while he was watching some of the other Avenues play football down in the park where we used to gather. He was sitting next to my brother, Al, and they hit him from the freeway, a lucky shot. He wasn't even actually in the gang—he just loved hanging out with us. This is just the one short block, maybe fifteen houses in all. I went to funeral after funeral after funeral after funeral.

Guns were easy to come by. There were guys in the neighborhood who broke into homes, and most of the homes had a gun somewhere. They were often junkies and needed to sell what they stole, and one of the easiest things to get rid of in our neighborhood was a gun. Even a TV was harder to sell. The guns, handguns at least, cost maybe twenty-five bucks, fifty bucks. I also had this one buddy, Winedrop, who used to repossess cars. At that time, a lot of people would keep their guns in their cars, and they were illegal guns, so when the car was repossessed, no one ever reported the loss of their illegal gun. My friend would repossess the cars and sell us the guns. There was never any shortage, that's for sure. Nor of bullets.

The first time I fired at somebody it wasn't a drive-by. I was with my father, who was doing tree-trimming and gardening side jobs to make some extra money. I would go with him, and I remember one time I was in hot water, so we had a .22 rifle in the back of the pickup truck he used. He was not a violent man, and he wasn't the kind who started anything, but he knew that his son's life was in danger. This was on Stadium Way over near Dodger Stadium. We were at a Chevron service station getting gas and there was a ballgame going on, so traffic was bumper to bumper. These guys from Cypress Park came along and they started firing at me. I picked up the rifle from the back of the truck and just emptied it into the car.

That was the first time I actually fired at somebody. My father was an old-fashioned kind of guy, but he knew this was a real dangerous gang. He was used to people having guns. He had always lived among people who had guns and used them, but usually not on one another.

I don't want you to think that I was a rebellious teenager, or misunderstood, or anything like that. I was neither Marlon Brando in *The Wild One* nor James Dean in *Rebel Without a Cause*. I didn't want to upset my father, and I didn't need to do crazy in front of him so that he would notice me. I knew he cared. Since he worked so much and I think because he didn't speak English, he was just not all that aware of what was going on. And I didn't confront him with my life. I didn't want him to know I was doing anything dangerous or illegal.

I f you were a gangbanger, there were two things that counted, and in a way they were the same thing. One of them was respect, as I said. If you felt that someone was not showing you the proper respect, that was a problem. It's not even about calling you names or insulting the gang. It might be something that most people wouldn't even notice, such as the way he looked at you or a comment he made about the shoes you were wearing.

The second thing was turf. The Avenues had their turf and no one else could use it without permission. In juvenile hall, they used to ask, "What are you guys fighting over?" We were fighting over turf, just like my dog guarding my yard. It's not his yard, but if you go near it, he'll defend it because it's his territory. We were like yard dogs— from the tracks to the freeway was our area, and everyone else had to stay out of it or we would attack them. It was such a waste.

It got personal very quickly. Sometimes a person had offended you, and sometimes you would just square off against somebody. Your two gangs were going at it, and sometimes you would just see somebody and think, *I'm going to get that guy* for whatever reason. I remember one guy was foolish enough to come down to our neighborhood when we were sitting out on the porch. That was how we marked our territory. We would sit at a house that was on one of the main streets—it was something about the traffic going by—and drink in the dark. Every neighborhood did this.

I was sitting out there one night with a bunch of guys and we had our rifles there, as we always did. This fool drove by with a couple of guys in his car, and what was really stupid was that he had a girl with him. I saw him, and when he came by the house, I opened up on the car. They were fortunate that no one died. Two of the guys and the girl got hit, but all of them survived. None of them was blinded or paralyzed; they were not permanently injured. I'm not proud of it, but that was the law of our jungle. I never dealt with him again. He went on banging and everything else, but I never saw that guy in my neighborhood again.

I remember this guy, he was a real gangster, who had said he was going to get me. One day I was standing in front of the house and he drove up in his car and said, "You're a dead man." I knew he was a serious man. When you grow up in that neighborhood, you know the serious people, the ones you have to take seriously. You know the blowhards who will never do anything but talk, but when a serious guy tells you, "Look, I'm coming for you. I'm gunning for you," you get ready and the best thing to do is strike first. He might have come after me after that—he might have been one of the ones who drove by one time and shot at the house. I don't know that, but we both knew that eventually there would be a showdown.

One day I was riding with a buddy and we saw this serious guy gassing up his car at the station on the corner of Pepper and Cypress.

I had my gun; I decided this was my opportunity. We went around the block, and as we pulled up at the pump next to the guy, I had the revolver in my hand. You can imagine the distance from one pump to the other, it's like nothing. I stepped out of the car and raised the gun to him. I remember his face. He froze; he could see his death. He knew it was too late to run, too late to pull his own gun, so he just froze with a look like *Oh my god*. I wasn't really thinking anything except about getting the job done—as far as I was concerned, it was my life or his.

I squeezed the trigger and it misfired. I squeezed it again and it misfired again. The gun was jammed. His faced changed when he realized he had been saved. I jumped back into the car and we drove off right away. You don't hang around. I'll always remember that guy, and I think to myself he must know how lucky he was, because he knew I was a serious guy too. His name was Eddie and he was in the Cypress Park gang. I always think about it and I'm glad that the gun misfired, I am. But remember, not only had this guy said he would get me, he was part of a gang that had killed people I grew up with, people I had partied with and fought with. I cared about these people a lot, and he was part of why they were dead. I just thought of it as payback. If it had been the other way around, he would have done the same thing. He would have killed me if he could have.

You continue that life, even though it's difficult, because it's difficult to get out of it. There were no options. You couldn't just be neutral, or a noncombatant, or mind your own business—unless you didn't want to leave your house ever. There was that option, but it meant that you had to take a lot of disrespect. If you decided to live that way, you moved out of the way when they walked down the hallway at school and used different water fountains to drink from. You swallowed your pride. That was not an option for me. For many, many of the guys, that was not an option. The way I lived as a youngster, I would be driving down the street and some guy would be double-parked, blocking the lane. I would honk a couple of times, but if he wouldn't move, I would get out of my car, go up to the guy's window, and reach in and start punching him. I felt I was owed some attention, some courtesy, and if this guy wouldn't show it to me, he deserved the consequences.

I started high school at Franklin Park High in Highland Park. I remember when I was in the tenth grade and the vice principal pulled me and couple of friends out of class to yell at us about something. Suddenly, one of my friends ran up and socked him on the chin. When you level the vice principal, that's something. Later, that vice principal took me aside and gave me the number of the Marine recruiting office. "You're not going to survive very long, living the way you do," he said. "Get out now, while you can."

I wasn't at Franklin long. In the spring of the first year, a carload of rival gangbangers saw Huero and me walking across the courtyard at school. They started shooting. Luckily they missed us, but shots shattered windows in a couple of the campus bungalows—that's what they were called—and almost hit a teacher. When they finally gave up and left, we were called down to the principal's office and told we were a hazard to the rest of the students. They decided to send us to a different school, somewhere where no one would know who we were.

They told us to come to Franklin every morning at five o'clock and get on a bus to go to a school in the San Fernando Valley. We weren't about to do that. Our neighborhood was our world. We found out that if you weren't living in the school district, they had no control over you anymore. So we just moved out of the school district. Huero had some relatives who lived in Arcadia, which is a pretty nice neighborhood. He moved in with them and transferred to Arcadia High School.

My brother had moved into his own apartment in El Sereno, so I went to school there, at Wilson High School, and that's where I finally graduated. It was actually kind of an achievement to graduate from high school. Most of the people I grew up with didn't. If you made it through junior high, you were lucky, but high school graduation? Never happened.

Wilson High had gangs, but I wasn't involved with any of them. I didn't have enemies, nor did I have any of my friends there; I was still a part of the Avenues, and every day after school I would ride the bus back to the neighborhood. I always had a gun at my waist, always. If the police came by while I was waiting for the bus, I would throw the gun in the bushes near the bus stop, but not too far away so that I could get it back before the bus came. They questioned me because they could see I was dressed as a gangbanger. Then later they got to know me, and they would say. "What's up, Night Owl?" and make conversation. The police were a constant part of our lives.

Everyone knew which bus I took, so anybody who wanted to kill me could watch for me there. I used to walk two or three blocks in one direction or another to avoid them. Sometimes I would see the car of a rival gang following the bus. Even though I had a gun, I didn't want to shoot it out with a carload of gangbangers, so I would jump off the bus early and duck into a stairway, whatever was close by, as long as I wasn't in their territory.

You lived a lifestyle and you didn't think about it; it became natural. For instance, when you pulled up to a light you never tailgated the guy in front of you in case someone spotted you and started shooting. You always left room so that you could pull out into the opposite lanes of traffic or onto the sidewalk. You never boxed yourself in.

Huero and I were getting arrested a lot, sometimes for minor violations, such as having an unregistered weapon or shoplifting, and sometimes for more serious things. Once during this time I was arrested for murder. We were driving through Highland Park about three in the morning. We'd been smoking PCP and got pulled over by the cops. They ordered us out of the car at gunpoint. They said a car fitting the description of ours had been the vehicle used in a drive-by earlier that night and someone had been killed. They arrested us, charged us with murder, and threw us into jail.

The death penalty had just been reinstated, like that day. As I sat in my cell, a cop came by and waved the newspaper with a headline about the death penalty in front of my face, telling me that that was what I had to look forward to. I guess he was trying to scare me, but it didn't really work. When it came time for them to examine me, they had me remove my shirt, and that's when they saw all my scars. They asked me how I got them and I said they were stab wounds. "So this is nothing new to you," one cop said. I thought, *This is it. I'm going to do some real time.* I still wasn't scared. I wasn't angry and I wasn't afraid. People were in and out of prison all the time. If it came down to being locked up for a long time, I'd be among friends.

We really hadn't done the drive-by, so the charges against us were dismissed, but this was the first time my dad became aware of what I was really doing, or the first time he felt he had to say something. When I got out my dad pulled me aside and said, "Hey, boy, what are you doing? You're going to spend your life in jail if you don't change your ways."

I told him, "Hey, it's not that bad. It's not such a big thing." I didn't want him to worry, but my response only made him more concerned because he could see I wasn't scared of going to jail. He was a good man, a kind man, and I knew he loved me. But there was nothing he could do to keep me from going my own way, and besides, he had his own life to worry about. He was working himself to death supporting two kids and sometimes a girlfriend. He rarely had a free moment or spare cash. I might not have known a lot back then, but I knew enough to realize I didn't want to go down that road for the rest of my life. So what could he say to me that would make any sense? "Be like me"? I don't think so. As far as I was concerned, belonging to a gang was the only way to avoid the life he'd found himself stuck in.

I continued to fight for my piece of turf. I did drive-bys and shoot-ups and wanted to make sure that people feared me. Along with the other Avenues I took up arms against a lot of competing gangs, like the Clover gang, Cypress Park, Frog Town. I was good at what I did and I knew it. Huero and I had both grown into serious tough guys who were never going to look back. I wouldn't have wanted to be on my shit list. A lot of people who were got hurt.

One Saturday night a bunch of us went to a party over on Fifty-second Street, believing it was an Avenues thing. It turned out to be a Cypress Park thing. No sooner did we enter through the back door—we always used the back entrance, the cool way to come and go—than a big fistfight broke out. It was complete mayhem. I had one guy up against a car doing a pretty good job on him when a flash of light at my side caught my attention. It was the streetlight reflecting off a knife as it was going into me. I felt a burning rip in my left side. He stabbed me several times. I turned around but he was too fast and managed to get away from me. As he ran away, just for the hell of it, he stuck the same knife in the back of another friend of mine, Randy "Chingus" Chavez.

After that the fight pretty much stopped. Probably people figured the cops would be there soon. I was bleeding pretty badly, but I thought, *It's just a wound. I'll survive.* My brother, Al, must have heard about the fight, because he pulled up to the house in his Monte Carlo, which he had just recently bought. Huero said, "You're going to the hospital." I said not to bother, that I would be fine. He wasn't hearing any of that, and luckily he was bigger than I was. He grabbed me by the sweatshirt and put me in the front seat of my brother's car. Huero jumped in the backseat and Al took off.

By now my sweatshirt was soaked with blood, and it was starting to spread onto the car seat. That bothered me. Blood was just pouring out of me, but my biggest worry was messing up the upholstery in my brother's new car. So I cupped my hands to scoop up the blood and started trying to throw it out the window. At the time I felt no pain. Now that I've learned something about the body, I know that I was probably in shock. The guy had actually hit an artery, and although I didn't know it then, I was bleeding to death, and not slowly.

So I was tossing the blood out the window for all I was worth, but after a while I started feeling really warm, which is not a good sign. We drove up to the guardhouse leading to the emergency-room ramp at County Medical, which we thought of as a ghetto hospital. I mean, we knew people who had been shot or stabbed, and when they went to County they died, so we figured that meant it was a bad hospital. Probably they would have died wherever they went. I found out later USC County had some of the best doctors in the area, but at the time we blamed the hospital. So as we pulled up to the emergency room, my brother said, "You could die here. Can you hold out till I get you to White Memorial?"

"Sure, let's go." What did I know? By the time we pulled up to White Memorial, I was feeling warm and light-headed. We got out of the car, and I couldn't walk. I ended up on my back in the emergency room, and they started to work on me while I was fading in and out. I remember coming to with this guy pushing hard on my side—I mean really *hard,* again and again. Now I know that he was putting a chest tube in me. When the lung cavity is penetrated, they want to be able to clear it, so they put a tube in between your ribs. And your ribs just aren't meant to be forced apart, they resist.

Finally, with one last big push, he got the tube between my ribs, and the pain was so awful that I passed out again. According to the police report, the last thing I said before I blacked out for good was, "Someone is gonna pay for this."

I woke up a week later. I was in the intensive care unit, and there was a tube down my throat and wires hooked up to me all over and I couldn't feel any part of my body. I couldn't move anything except my eyes, probably because of medication. I opened them and turned them to the side, and there was the priest from the local Catholic church. I thought, *Goddamn, I'm gonna die.*

I faded out again, and for the next few days I would fade in and out of consciousness. Every time I woke up, there was someone else there—not only my brother and my father, but relatives from Texas and everywhere else and I thought, *Oh shit, this has to be serious. They wouldn't be here if I wasn't dying.* But I wasn't. After about a week, I started to feel better. One day a nurse said, "OK, now try to stand up against the bed," and I was incredibly happy. I thought this was the greatest thing in the world, I guess because it meant I really was going to recover.

In fact, I had nearly died, and if it wasn't for Huero I would have bled to death. So Huero saved my life. He came over to see me my first night home. He was mad, mad about what happened to me, so he had gotten an old Western-style revolver—the kind with the cylinder that holds the bullets. But every time he shot it, the cylinder popped out. That didn't stop him. He drove to where I was stabbed and shot up the house with his broken gun. Five years later, the guy who stabbed me was found dead on the side of a highway in Arizona. Someone had killed him. I have no idea who or why, but a part of me wishes I had had the opportunity to settle that score myself.

When I was well enough, I got a job washing dishes at County Medical, of all places. I had to lie about my age to get it, but nobody really cared as long as I had a pair of hands and was willing. I was still recovering from the stabbing, and I thought that having a job would be a way to fill the time. I didn't like to do nothing. I worked from three in the afternoon until midnight, and it was close to school, so I could still go to class when I wanted to. I worked there full time for a couple of years, and I thought it was the greatest money in the world. They had a credit union, insurance, things like that. I thought all this was fantastic. It's funny, isn't it? Even though I stole anything I needed and was a respected member of a very tough gang, I still liked this middle-class life. It was like I lived in two worlds.

Just before I graduated, I started to see a woman named Sybil. I liked her, but she was not much different from any of the other women I went around with, except for one thing. She got pregnant. Sybil and I separated before Little Rubes—Ruben Jr.—was even born. There was no chance of us getting married and settling down; it was just not going to work out. I wasn't at the hospital when he was born, on September 20, 1977. I was in Mexico. I remember that they brought Little Rubes down to Mexico so that I could see him, but I'd contracted typhoid fever and I was sick as a dog the whole time they were there. He lived with his mother for a time after he was born, but I saw him whenever I could, made sure he had what he needed. Any money I could spare went to him.

Sybil and I get along as friends now. She has a responsible job with Kaiser Permanente, the big health-insurance company. In fact, we were just talking a little while ago about what property of ours Little Rubes could inherit. We're friendly enough that we can sit and talk about what we're going to do and what's the best move, while I have some time left.

I wanted Little Rubes with me. I'd seen too many kids beat up by their stepfather or their mother's new boyfriend. I vowed that my son would never live through that. So he spent a lot of time with me even when he was very young, but he had to fit into my life. I so clearly remember being in the front yard, mowing the lawn or watering or something, and Little Rubes in one of those motorized swings that goes back and forth and plays music. He loved that swing. So he was in the swing, but I was always worried about drive-bys or some other kind of attack, so I had an assault rifle leaning up against the fence. I know it sounds crazy to have an assault rifle when my son is right beside me, but I felt I had no choice.

I still had a temper. I still needed to be sure I was respected. I wasn't really part of a gang after I graduated from high school, but I still had the gang mentality. One time I was at a barbecue in the park and this guy did something I didn't like. He was not one of the Avenues, and we had a disagreement, but there were families around and I didn't want to cause trouble in front of the kids. I don't even remember the words now. The words were not important, just his attitude. Again, what might seem disrespectful to me might mean nothing to you.

Anyway, he made me angry, and since I couldn't settle it right there, I said, "OK, down the road I will run into you again and we will talk it over. If you come out straight and tell me, 'Look, it was a mistake,' no problem. If you give me this attitude again, then we will have to handle it." I'm not the kind of guy to go after someone. They might say something in the wrong way or act like they're better than I am, but I don't immediately pull out my gun.

So we went our separate ways, and I don't know how he felt about it. He might not have realized that I was speaking very seriously. About three months passed, and I didn't forget this guy and the barbecue. I wasn't angry; you must remember, it's not about anger, it's more like a debt of honor that must be settled one way or the other. Say someone owes you money. You don't wake up every morning and think, *I'm going to get my money back from that son of a bitch.* But it's at the back of your mind, and you know you're going to have to deal with the situation.

This is just a part of who I am, and now I know that, so I try not to put myself in situations where I might feel the need to settle a score. But you can imagine that today, when I'm riding with my Mongol colors on and the police pull me over for no reason—really no reason at all except that I'm a Mongol—and they curse me and say they're going to get me . . . well, that is very frustrating for me. That is very difficult. The same when people make these ridiculous charges about what the Mongols do and don't do.

But I'm ahead of my story. The point is that, about three months later, I was driving down Whittier Boulevard and I saw the guy sitting in his car. I stopped, got out of my car, and went over to speak to him. I told him very clearly, "I didn't like what you said and the way you said it." If the guy had said that it was a misunderstanding, I would have shaken hands with him and left. He did not. He said, more or less, "Fuck you, I don't care what you think." I was already pretty worked up, but that sent me into a rage, and I pulled my gun out and shot him, twice. I thought I'd hit him in the face, and I thought I'd probably killed him.

I was already on probation for some other small deal, but I knew that I had to leave town. There were witnesses, and I felt pretty certain that he was dead. My father suggested I go and stay with some of our relatives down in Mexico for a while. So one night I caught a train and rode down to Laredo and crossed the Rio Grande to Nuevo Laredo, to my grandfather's house.

It was a very different world there. There was a different atmosphere, people were different, there were no gangs (at least not that I knew of then). I'd become too used to the streets, though, and I felt a little trapped. In addition to his house in town, my grandfather had a small ranch outside town in the scrub, where he would go hunting.

I got a little restless, and one day when my grandfather was out, I took his .22 rifle and a box of shells and wrapped the gun in a box so it looked like it was a vacuum cleaner. Actually people there carried guns all the time, but I was so used to hiding things that I tried to disguise that rifle. The ranch was very far, really way out. You had to take a bus to the end of the line, and then you would go down a small dirt road. At the very end of the road was my grandfather's ranch.

It had a one-room house with a fireplace and an old wagon in the front yard, the kind of thing you might see at an antique shop in Los Angeles. But my grandfather used that wagon to gather firewood still. There was a sack of rice and a sack of beans and some canned goods and an endless supply of wildlife to feed on. I had never skinned and cleaned a rabbit before, but I had heard my grandfather and my uncles talking about it, and when you're really hungry you figure these things out. I stayed there for a couple of months by myself. It was an incredible place to be, especially for a guy who had been in the city for a dozen years. Completely quiet, no sign of people at all. At night I would sleep outside in that wagon and stare at all the stars. Of course at the same time I was wondering what my homeys were doing at that moment. It took my grandfather forever to figure out where I was, and when he did he came and brought me back. He was furious. The last thing I remember him telling me was that I was a hopeless case, but that bounced right off me. I was ready to go back to L.A. anyway. I had decided to give myself up to get back to my real life.

When I reported back to my probation officer, he said nothing about the shooting. They gave me short time in the county jail for violating probation, but that was it. Later my friends told me that the guy had actually survived the shooting. I sometimes wonder how badly he was hurt, if he has sinus problems or if his eyesight was affected.

I know that it was nothing that totally handicapped him because I heard that he was back on the streets, though I never saw him again. Even though I never officially left the gang—no one does—I wasn't hanging around with the Avenues anymore.

After I got out of jail, I found a job in a frozen-fish warehouse in Pasadena, where I learned to drive a forklift. Eventually the owner taught me how to make shrimp and crab cocktails for packaging and shipping. Most every night when it was quitting time, a couple of the other guys and I would take some shrimp and crabs, start a small fire in the back, and cook us up a feast. I also worked for a mason and learned how to lay bricks. I had lots of odd jobs and somehow managed to keep myself more or less together.

I was not really part of the Avenues anymore, but I was still in and out of jail. There were a lot of little arrests, like if I got into a fight in a bar and hit a guy with a beer mug or a bottle, all of a sudden you have assault with a deadly weapon. And I might be carrying a gun at the same time. Once Al and I were pulled over in Montebello, and because we were who we were, they searched the Volkswagen and found the two .45s that we had in the trunk. What was different that time is that the case was thrown out of court. The court said the search was illegal. We even got the weapons back— now *that* was unusual.

I did weekends for a while in the old county jail. Weekends is when you're basically a working citizen, maybe with a wife and kids, but you like to go out drinking with your buddies on the weekends. That makes you a little careless and you get arrested for driving drunk three or four times. And that means you have to do some time. A judge doesn't want you driving around drunk every weekend, and he wants to teach you a lesson, but he doesn't want to destroy your life, since you're a productive citizen. So the judge might give you two years of weekends. Every Friday for the next two years you report to the jail and check in. Every Monday morning you are released and you go to work. The weekend prisoners don't mix with the regular prisoners. At that time—it may not be that way now—I went to the old county jail up on Temple. That's where the Manson family was held for a while, but by the eighties, it was being used for weekend time.

It wasn't that bad. I never had better access to drugs than I did there, and they were the best, that's the truth. You could get hallucinogens and uppers, and downers that would put you to sleep. I would get loaded and sleep for the two days and dream about women and by Monday not even realize that I had been in there. I never had to bring the drugs in because everyone else had them. I just bought what I wanted.

The problem with coming back to the same world you left is that you can't just say, "Time out, I'm not a gangbanger anymore. Leave me alone." In all these organizations, whether it's a street gang or a motorcycle club, you need to prove yourself, but once you've earned your place, you can't just give it up. For one thing, the reputation is there. I had such a reputation that punks could make a reputation by taking me out. I would say I have always been a prime target. It's like the military, I guess; the best thing to do is to hit an enemy officer, because he has the experience, and losing an officer hurts morale. On the other hand, there are always new recruits who take on the really tough jobs. They want to prove themselves. If you've earned your spot, no one is going to make you participate. So while you're still taking part in the gang, you're not always on the front lines.

As long as you're living in the neighborhood, you're still in the mess. You still eat at the same restaurants and shop in the same places. I always had people threatening me, my house was always being shot at, and the police were always raiding us. They would come at two o'clock in the morning and kick the door down. Then they'd search the house for weapons and take any they found. Now to us this was all routine. You live with a gun at your waist whether you are going to the restaurant on the corner or catching the bus.

Mexico became my escape hatch from that life. I began to go down there more often. My grandfather wouldn't have me back, so the next time I went for a long visit, I stayed at Uncle Hector's house in Guadalajara. I just went down to hang out with his family for a while until things cooled off in the neighborhood, and they were very welcoming. My cousins would take me downtown, and I enjoyed seeing this beautiful old Mexican city. After a while, my cousins and uncles started to talk to me about what I was doing in the United States. They said I was a bright kid and I should do something with myself other than getting into trouble—not that they even knew the half of it.

At first they told me I should study medicine to become a doctor, but I really didn't see myself doing that. Even in Mexico, where things are a little easier, it would take so many years of school, and I didn't really have the basics. I just didn't want to do it.

But they took me down to the University of Guadalajara, and I hung out with some of my cousins and they showed me around the campus. A lot of those relatives were doctors or in the medical profession, so they had bought a little duplex in Guadalajara where they could stay while they were attending classes. They told me about radiology, and I was kind of interested in it—the X-rays and what the lab techs do. So they got me some books and they just kept telling me I could do this. I started looking at the books, and they let me sit in on a few classes, and I began to feel that I actually could do it. *Firme,* I thought, which is Spanish slang, a word that means "solid" and we used to mean "great."

Next thing I knew I was signed up for a radiology course and taking classes. I had to refresh my memory about math and learn some things I hadn't. My uncle paid for a tutor for me. They gave me enough training to work as a radiologic technologist. I liked the classes and I liked running around with my cousins, and I ended up passing enough tests to do an internship, where I would have hands-on experience. I seemed to catch on pretty well, and I liked doing the actual work.

It's like they got me to do the whole course piece by piece without telling me what was actually going on. So finally they said, "Look, you're qualified to take the test to become a licensed radiologic technologist. Why don't you do it?" So I did, and I got licensed in Mexico. It didn't mean much to me then, because I knew I wasn't going to live in Mexico. Weeks after I passed the test, I was back in East L.A.

4

Graduate Studies

When I came back from Mexico with my new radiologic technologist certificate, I didn't do anything with it at first, but I read about radiology some more, along with the subjects I liked—history and science, mainly. I was still in my early twenties, and I still had the gang mentality. I worked odd jobs, hung out with my friends from the old neighborhood, and was still in and out of the county jail. I have said that you are always a member of your gang, but it's also true that the gang doesn't really leave you either. It's part of you.

As far as that goes, the police don't let you leave the gang either. Whether you're gangbanging or not, they still hassle you. I was pulled over and searched more times than I can count. Since there were people who were still out to get me, I still had to carry a gun, and I would get busted for that. So even if I wasn't doing drive-bys anymore, even if I wasn't doing the gang's business, I wasn't allowed to leave that world. I was in and out of the county jail, and once in a bar I got into a fight with a guy while I was carrying a gun, so I was charged with assault with a deadly weapon.

There wasn't much I could do at the time. I was given a public defender and had to agree to a deal on the plea. I bargained it down to short time, some of it in North County Correctional Facility—which everybody called Wayside, from its original name. What really hurt was that I had to leave my son. I knew that I didn't want him to see me locked up, so I would be out of his life for years.

In a way, this was my college in gladiator school. Though I was not so much an active participant, I saw some things there that taught me just how far human beings could go. Wayside is in Castaic, a city about sixty-five miles north of Los Angeles, pretty much out in the middle of nowhere. You get a cell in a dormitory with maybe sixteen other bunks, as compared to other prisons, where the cells are about six feet by eight feet, with bunk beds, a stainless steel toilet—because they're easier to clean and you can't break them easily—and a sink. There are a couple of little shelves where you can put your belongings. In other words, there's no such thing as privacy. You become accustomed to your cellmate using the toilet in front of you (which is why the cells are well ventilated). You lose all that kind of modesty. Maybe outside you slept with the lights off, but in prison there's always a light on and you adapt to it. You adapt to a lot.

Although I never did hard time in prison, a lot of my homeys did, and prison is not a place I wanted to be. There were three floors—tiers, they're always called—with a lounge area down below where you can play cards or bullshit for an hour or two a day, if they let you. When you are locked up in a two-man cell for twenty or twenty-one hours a day, you really look forward to talking to anybody. But if they consider you one of the leaders of a gang, a shot-caller, they don't want you socializing with the others and you can be locked down for twenty-three hours a day.

I was in solitary confinement once for a while, after a fistfight. The guards don't really care about fights. They just say, "Both of you guys go to the hole." I went to the hole, and it's not all that bad. The worst part is that you don't have anybody to talk to. I was there for twenty or thirty days, but there are guys who go in for six months. To the average person this might be an unbearable kind of punishment, but remember being locked up itself wasn't a big deal to me. I was already locked up—the only thing different with solitary is that I had one less guy to talk to.

You carry around one of those brown accordion folders where you keep all your court documents. It's called your paperwork, and you're entitled to it because technically you can continue to fight your case. But it ends up being kind of like your passport and your ID. And not only for the administration—the other inmates want to know who you are and what you're all about. So you keep it in your cell and you carry it with you when you move from cell to cell, prison to prison. If people don't already know who you are and want to find out, you can show them your paperwork. Asking to look at somebody's papers was not considered rude, as long as you're not asking someone who's important. I might still have some of mine; the last time the Feds raided us they took a lot of that paperwork, but I did find an arrest sheet they'd missed.

Some people have a hard time with being locked up, some don't. It depends on what your lifestyle was outside and what really pushes your buttons. It wasn't the end of the world for me. I didn't think the food was that bad, you can watch TV if you can afford to have one sent to you, you can read. If you have money you can buy things or somebody on the outside can purchase things for you. There are companies where your family members can go to order a TV, food, or magazines. But you have to go through these companies so that the facility knows that no weapons or drugs or anything else are concealed inside. I had a little TV. The prison didn't have cable, but they had a way of hooking it up so I could get reception.

You talk, you read, you write letters. I got to keep up with the outside world there more than I did when I was outside. I read newspapers, but if for some reason there's something that the authorities didn't want the inmates to read, they cut it out. I guess they'd cut something that could incite a riot—maybe a story about a riot in a prison. Of course they read your letters before they sent them out. If you had mail coming in, they took the letter out of the envelope and checked it with special lights that let them see through the envelope and the stamp. Back then people used to try to sneak in LSD on the back of a postage stamp, since all you need is a tiny little drop of acid to get off. They stopped that by taking off all the stamps.

I spent a lot of my time exercising. If you let yourself go when you do time, if you don't care about your hygiene or your fitness or anything else, that makes time go by a lot slower and a lot harder. You have to tell yourself, *I'm in here and I've got to make the best of this.* They stopped allowing weights because the guards became afraid that the inmates were building themselves up too much, becoming "supercriminals." I did sit-ups, push-ups, pull-ups, whatever I could. If you don't, you're going to go nuts. If you do, you feel a lot better.

If you act right and you don't screw up and they don't catch you fighting or hiding a knife in your cell, you can get a job. They had a dairy farm at Wayside—you could learn to milk cows if you wanted—but I wasn't much of a farmer, so I kept away from that. You can do yard work, clean up the place, do laundry, work in the kitchen. I didn't mind laundry. I like to keep busy.

I had visitors—my father and Al, and some of the women I knew.

But it was routine among the other guys for their wives and girl-friends to stop visiting, and they would just adjust to that. I can't say it didn't bother them, but they didn't get real angry about it either. Either they had bigger problems to deal with or they just decided to deal with it when they got out. But the saddest were the people in there who had no one at all, not even anyone who had left them. They couldn't get a dollar; they couldn't even buy a Snickers bar.

There were always drugs. Metal detectors only detect metal, so powder and drugs can still get by. Sometimes the guards would co-operate. There are honest guards, but there are some crooked ones too. Those guards can be paid off with money or with sex. A guy's woman is willing to have sex with the guard in return for letting the drugs in. The media turns it into "sexual slavery," but it's not. Let's face it; sex for some women is not a big deal. It may be how they make their living. Everyone knows it goes on a lot.

You can also smuggle the drugs in, putting them in different cavities of your body. There are people who will bring them in by concealing the drugs in a balloon up their butt. It's called a keister. Someone who needs drugs and knows that he's going to be sentenced to a year the next day would go ahead and push all that shit up his butt. I never needed it that much.

Every once in a while they would order a shakedown. All of a sudden the doors open and they make you get out and stand against the wall while they turn your cell inside out. They have a dog sniffing for drugs; they lift your mattresses, squeeze your toothpaste. It works sometimes if the inmates aren't expecting it: they'll find a weapon, a knife, some drugs. You get used to it.

You can get some exercise out in the yard for two to three hours a day, depending on whether there were problems going on in the prison or not. You needed to be careful not to step into another group's territory—there were the Black Guerillas and the Aryan

Brotherhood—and you stay out of one another's corners. As long as you do that, there usually isn't a problem. Even though you had to be careful outside, I still wanted to get there, even though I had the option of staying in. It's amazing how much you can hunger for the sunshine and the air, even the grass or the dirt, anything, after being locked up inside for months and months. You want to go out there even if you know it's safer in your cell.

Some poor guys get beat up because they've never been locked up and don't know how to act. Some white guy who thinks it's cool to talk to Hispanics or black guys—he's got a problem. The blacks and Hispanics will look at him like *Get the fuck out of here.* In addition, his own people are going to teach him the rules, and he might end up with a couple of bruised ribs and swollen eyes. They will teach him not to fraternize with other groups.

Race is everywhere in prison; it dictates so much of how you act. The groups set rules that you can't associate with the other races. Blacks will tell other blacks you can't associate with the whites or Hispanics and the Hispanics do the same. So tensions build up and because tensions build up you stick to yourself and because you stick to yourself tensions build up. It's really a mess.

There are usually a few people who try to be spokesmen for their race, but there isn't much they can say beyond telling people just to stay out of one another's way. That's hard to do in a cell, or any-where else, really—there just aren't that many places to go. You go to the restroom in the lounge and there's five of another color in there blocking the mirror or the sinks when you want to wash your hands. They don't want to move because that might seem like they are afraid of you; you want to prove that you're not afraid. So you push your way in and that's where it happens.

I didn't do drugs, and I tried to keep from mixing with the gangs. I wanted to do my time and get out and see my son. I knew a lot of people in there from the gangs, some from the Avenues, although when you are in there you don't make a big deal of the gang you're from. I would see members of some of the rival gangs, and we would just ignore one another. But of course because I was Hispanic, I was a *soldado,* a soldier with La eMe, the Mexican mafia. Every gang member automatically becomes a soldier for La eMe, and I would never go against the grain.

Originally, La eMe—the name is just the way of spelling out "M" in Spanish—was a good idea, I think, but now it has hurt the Hispanic community. In the beginning, it was formed by Hispanics to protect themselves in prison. Until La eMe was formed, the Hispanics were at a disadvantage. They were getting beaten or robbed all the time. La eMe provided protection. If you were Hispanic—whether you were a respected gangbanger or just a lone guy—and someone started to beat on you, all the other Hispanics were going to jump in. It was intimidation, as much as anything, but it worked. Then the people running La eMe realized that it had gotten so successful at creating fear that they didn't have to stop at the prison gate. Even when the gangbangers are back out on the street they have to answer to La eMe because sooner or later they would end up inside again. So La eMe could make dope dealers and certain kinds of businesses give them money. The idea of self-defense turned into something that was just about greed.

You don't join La eMe. There is no initiation; it just happens. Basically you're a part of it because if anything happens, if a riot happens between the blacks, whites, or the Asians you automatically take part with your race, so in a sense you're a soldier whether you want to be or not. It is run by the bosses, the shot-callers, who are mostly in Pelican Bay, which is the most secure prison in California, a supermax facility. Everyone there is in solitary confinement all the time, but there is still communication, both ways, and they are the ones who make the big decisions. They get their messages out in code, through drawings, on a white handkerchief or the little plastic cups we used. There are inmates who can draw incredible things. They'll etch the artwork there to create an Aztec picture with a code. Hit lists and contracts. The prison actually has people who try to break the codes.

La eMe is broken down like an army: there are the generals at the top and the *soldados* underneath them. In any individual prison, you have a sergeant in charge. These are not their titles formally, it's just a way of describing the organization. Every little block of cells has a guy in charge of it, and he'll make sure everyone stays in line. There are a lot of rules as to how you behave. For instance, you can't ask to get transferred without getting permission from whoever is in charge of your module. You have a guy who's in charge of your fitness; he's usually one of the well-built guys and he puts the whole module through training. Every morning you do calisthenics or sit-ups. Personal hygiene and grooming are very important.

Like in the neighborhood, respect is everything and disrespect could happen in many ways—from not obeying an order to go and handle something, for instance, to the way you talk to somebody. What you might think is not a big deal to somebody else can be the worst disrespect possible in this situation. It's *Hey, who do you think you are* and W*ho in the fuck do you think I am?* You could be in line for food and the guy in front of you hasn't gotten a spoon yet. If you reach around him to grab a spoon, he might think that is the worst disrespect in the world. He could turn right around and do something then and there or he can hold it inside. It's amazing how guys can hold this stuff in. A week might pass and the guy doesn't seem any different toward you, but one day you're in the yard and he'll come at you. You don't even remember what he's so mad about. But inside, this guy feels you disrespected him.

Anything could trigger some of those hotheads, but the head person for La eMe would have to approve any punishment. When the head orders a beating, he will say someone needs to be touched up. A killing is called "hard candy."

In the old prisons, you had blind spots, which could be a stairway where they can't see you or a corner where there's a water fountain cut into a niche. That's where a lot of stuff happens, such as beatings, stabbings, intimidation. They'll catch you near a stairway where a deputy can't see and you can get the shit kicked out of you. It never happened to me. I knew a lot of people and as long as you fight back you stand a chance. I got into a couple of scuffles but never anything bad. The rule is simple: You need to stand up for yourself or they will take advantage.

But there were guys who fell into the trap of La eMe because they wanted to earn respect or they wanted to make a name for themselves. They would volunteer. Now, the shots are usually called by people who have been in a long time, so long that they don't give a shit what happens. Unfortunately they pull in the guys who aren't doing that long a stretch. They get them into this mess and they wind up adding another few years on to their time.

There are even suicide missions. If they definitely want to send their message, they send a suicide mission. Someone might be assigned to do a hit when the deputy opens a cell door. His job is to rush in the cell and kill the inmate and face the consequences. If the guards decide to shoot, then you'll die in the attempt. Even if they don't shoot, you have stabbed somebody in front of witnesses. That's why you usually try to do it without getting caught.

Say you are in a module with blacks, whites, and Hispanics, twenty or thirty of each. When something was going to happen—let's say between Hispanics—the Hispanics in charge will yell "bunk status," and all the whites and the Asians would rush to their cells and lie on their bunks facedown so that they couldn't see what was going on. This happened whenever anything needed to be handled, not just for a fight. It would have to be more serious than that, usually when they were going to give somebody hard candy. That way there were no witnesses as to who stabbed who. If they caught you watching during bunk status, then you would get it too.

I never had to go to bunk status because the Hispanics called most of the bunk status, so I never had to go lie facedown. When the blacks or whites had to take care of business, we never gave a shit. We might go sit down and look the other way, but they didn't have the same control we did. I'm sure it didn't make them happy.

Hard candy was handled through stabbings, with shanks. There are just so many ways of making weapons. Maybe a bunk has a loose piece of metal; a guy will break it off and sharpen it on cement. I have seen some gruesome shanks, but there are sweeps all the time and they're looking for stuff like that, so they clean them out a lot, but they can't eliminate them. You can lock me in a room, and unless it's a cement room with nothing in it, I will find something there that you can make into a weapon.

Sometimes the best you have is a toothbrush filed into a point or a nail hooked into something else. A nail in the chest or the belly is not going to do a hell of a lot, but you can get your target in the neck or you can take his eye out, both eyes. The thing about it is that you don't have much time. So what you do is you go for the most vulnerable area, the throat or the face. You may not kill him, but you're going to leave him with a serious message. So you go for the throat and the eyes.

I saw this happen.

Even though I knew about these things, I was not involved with any of it. If you're a respected guy, you may not have to take on any of that stuff and you will still be treated with respect by the guy who's running things. After all, I knew the rules already. I didn't have to be told what to do or how to act, but I wanted nothing to do with it. It's a minefield, and that's the reason most of them turn on their brothers. Almost every member of La eMe that I have known has had them turn on him. It's an unforgiving business, but basically they kill one another, not civilians. If someone had a problem they would have to get the green light to kill someone, unless it was really a blatant violation of the rules. No one would blame you for killing someone who was a snitch, for instance, or if you were running around with another group that you shouldn't be running with. In these kinds of cases, everybody knows you're way out of line.

But they policed their own. La eMe took care of disputes between the prisoners. If you were having a problem with another inmate, they would look into it and they might say, "Hey, you two guys want to rough it up, go ahead. You got five minutes, go to the back, no weapons." Everything is timed. When someone says stop, you had to stop or everyone would jump you and beat you up. So they had some degree of control over things.

The guards, in fact, are not much better than La eMe in some ways. A lot of law enforcement seems to enjoy this gladiator mentality. When La eMe was going to do something, the guards would come up to me with a big smile and say, "Oh man, it's gonna happen now," or "Here we go, it's the big one." From their point of view it was just two groups that they couldn't stand and they were about to kill each other. People don't want to think this happens, but in 1998, guards at Corcoran State Prison were indicted by the Justice Department for setting inmates against each other, basically just like two gladiators fighting it out in the Roman Colosseum, for the guards' amusement. That's why they call it gladiator school.

The thing about guards that amazes me is that when they fail at their job, people get killed, but the guards get rewarded instead of fired. They complain that they don't have enough staff to prevent killings, so more deputies are brought in, and that's what they want, to make their work easier. But it's not about staff. I've watched three, four, or five of them sitting there talking about their boats and the weekend. One guy got killed while a couple of them were reading the paper and drinking coffee. In fact, the problem is that no one is there to make sure they're doing their job correctly. No one is there to crack the whip. Prisoners would be ordered to be released but it would be two days before they got out, because at every step the guards give you trouble and you can't complain or they'll throw you right back in the cell. In the county jail they don't rehabilitate you, they just lock you up.

On the other hand, the guards had to be careful, because there were people there who just didn't give a fuck. These guys impressed even me at how stone-faced they could be. In prison, you know that if you beat up a guard, you're going to get the shit kicked out of you. You're locked up in their world, and it's not like there are paramedics. They can lay you out and you can be there for hours or days if they want to leave you. You could end up in the hospital in a coma. I mean, you couldn't call your lawyer and say, "I beat up a guard and they broke both my arms. What are you going to do about it?"

But I met people in there who would look at the guards and say, "Fuck you. Let's do it. Come on in this cell." I had a hard life, but some people in there totally amazed me. Sometimes the guards would beat them up, but sometimes all they could do was say something like, "As long as you don't touch me, you can talk all the shit you want." In reality, they were just saying, *I don't want to go in there.* Some of these inmates reminded me of a cat, because they were always so aware of everything. And even when they come out, they don't lose that. That's one reason why some of those guys get killed so fast on the outside. They are used to living that lifestyle, so they're always pulling out their guns. And these guys always carry a gun, always!

There are dirty guards in every prison, and they will do things for drugs and sex, depending on what turns them on. But the thing about it is that no one will ever see it other than the people who actually go to prison. The reason we can see it is because the guards know that we aren't going to testify against anybody, not even them. The system works that way. They know that we know, but that we will keep our mouths shut. After all, you have friends from your gang who are in there for life. If you cause any trouble, they might be the ones punished for it.

So the guards, a lot of them, just do whatever they want. Say you're a white guy and you get into an argument with a black, and you call him a fuckin' nigger. If a black guard overhears you, he may leave you in a vulnerable area the next time a situation comes up. He might just leave a gate open next time and let the blacks get to you.

I saw a riot at Wayside between the Hispanics and blacks. It's funny, it had to do with fashion. When you're locked up, they give you jeans, but not all of them are exactly the same. Some of them are real gangster jeans, really baggy and with a red line down the side. They used to hand out these pants, and you would fold them up real neat and put them between the mattress and the metal bunk. Then you slept on them—to iron them, so when you went out the next day, you had your hard-core blue jeans. So when you saw an especially good pair you would try to grab them from the laundry guy. Otherwise you could end up with jeans that were three times too small for you.

The way the riot started was when a Hispanic guy had a pair of red-line jeans and a black guy got them. I don't know how he got hold of them, but that's how the whole riot started, over a pair of jeans. You could feel the riot coming; you just knew it was tense. It all flared up outside at the dairy farm, so the next thing you know the guys were chasing one another with shovels and rakes. They supplied us with little construction hard hats, so people were running around with hard hats, beating on one another. No one was killed, but many people went to the hospital after being hit with a shovel. I was in maximum security at the time, but I could see people through the windows chasing one another. It was even kind of entertaining in a weird way. We had music piped into the cell, and I was sitting there watching while they all kind of moved to the song.

While I was locked up there were people who were fingered as snitches and dealt with. This was not usually paranoia, either; the prisoners have good sources. Prisoners work in the office and they have access to just about all the files. Now, with computers and Internet access, they can get even more information. They have access to all this information and the guards don't give a crap. Before a new inmate even gets there they will already know who he is and what he did and all about him. Some guys are basically dead on arrival, if they have it coming to them.

I did my time and tried to make it bearable. You give up hope—not to the extent that you would let yourself die, but you stop thinking about getting out and just get on with it and make it as comfortable as you can. Nobody tries to escape except in the movies. You just hold on to the fact that you're going to get out. You have to forget about how much time you have or how much longer it's going to be before you get out. If you spent all your time thinking about that, you would drive yourself crazy. Of course, when you find yourself with just a couple of months left, then you get kind of antsy, but even so, you can't be thinking about each day.

I have heard of people trying to commit suicide by hanging themselves or throwing themselves off a top tier because they couldn't deal with it anymore. Those are the people who sat there and thought about it and said, *Oh man, I got three years* and *I've been here two days and I don't like it*, instead of giving themselves time to adapt to the situation. If they had given it time they would've adapted.

Then there are others who get so they like prison. I grew up with guys who would get out and then go right back in. I used to think, *What's wrong with that bonehead?* After I went through it, I realized that it was where those guys wanted to be. They got three meals a day and a place to sleep. They didn't have to worry about the tax man or the mortgage. You and I have to worry where our next dollar is going to come from, but these guys didn't have any of those worries. Unless they get out there and stay out, and then all of a sudden everyone has moved on and passed them by. That's sad too.

I met some interesting people locked up. In fact, just about everybody in there has had an interesting life. Not that they're innocent; that's mostly only in movies. I do know innocent people who have been sent away, but most of the people are in for a reason.

I haven't been back in there since I got out in 1995.

I really didn't think about what I was going to do when I got out. Believe it or not, it was not a major thing to me. Things hadn't changed much in the neighborhood when I got back. A couple of my homeys picked me up in their truck, and I wanted to get Little Rubes a present but didn't have any money yet. We decided to go to Jack in the Box for lunch. I was in the back of the truck as we went to the drive-through window. In those days they used to have the actual jack-in-the-box heads as decoration, and I was sitting next to it as they were ordering. I looked at that jack-in-the-box head and I thought, *Wow, wouldn't that look cool in my son's room.*

So I stood up and I wrapped my arms around this head and started wrestling with it. The person at the window stuck her head out and her mouth dropped open. The guys were laughing, and finally I snapped off the head and they just took off, and as we drove away the girl just looked. We didn't even get our burgers. I was going to make a night-light out of it for Rubes's room. I still have that head in the attic, but maybe now Jack in the Box will want it back.

I saw Little Rubes pretty often, and I'd take him places and do things my way. We would go to parks and playgrounds and go on the swings. I tried to be a regular dad as much as I could, you know, as long as being public enemy number one didn't get in the way.

My life was changing, though. I was taking care of Little Rubes more, and he was very important to me. And I was losing friends. One of my good friends in the Avenues was my buddy Randy, the one who was stabbed when I was. One night he went out on a drive-by very near where I lived on Ulysses with a friend named Curly. But when they got to the house, the gangbangers there had their guns ready, and they decided to shoot it out. All four tires of Randy's car were blown out, but he kept on driving, and he got as far as the Nightingale Junior High parking lot before the car gave out. Curly said, "Let's get out of here," but Randy had been smoking angel dust and decided, I guess, to try to fix his tires. That was his big mistake, because the people from the house had chased him all the way to the school. He was alone when they caught up with him. He must have known he was going to die before they killed him. When we got there the next day, my buddy's blood was all over the parking lot.

Then one day Huero was driving down the street and somebody from a rival gang shot him. The bullet went in under his armpit and lodged in his heart, but he kept driving. He was very close to his mom, and he drove all the way home. I remember afterward his mom crying and telling me, "He had pulled up to the front of the house. I was on the porch and he stopped the car and looked up at me and smiled. Then his head hit the steering wheel." Huero must have been about twenty-five years old when he died.

It was hard to lose him. It's the only time I can remember crying. We had known each other since we were kids. We used to sit in front of my house and talk about everything in the world. He saved my life. He was the first guy who would pick up a weapon when I got hurt. I do know who killed him. I didn't do anything myself, but someone handled it.

Anyway, enough of my people had died that I had to be aware that sometime my luck was going to run out. I didn't make a conscious decision about changing my life, but I met some guys at a party who were working as radiologic technologists, and they said I should give it a try. So I went downtown and filled out the forms and had to take a test with a lot of other people. And to my own surprise, I passed the test.

To my even bigger surprise, I got a job very easily. I found out later that there was a terrific shortage of RTs in California at the time, and I found work right away. This was the first time that ever happened to me. I found a job at County Medical, working nights, but there were many other clinics in the area that also needed an RT. I could walk into a clinic and show them my certificate and they would say, "You can start today. How much do you want?"

I had my dad's work ethic, so I would work all night at the hospital and then go to a clinic about eight thirty or nine and work there until nine or nine thirty at night. I was in such demand that they didn't care if I slept while I was there. If I didn't have a patient for thirty or forty minutes, I could take a nap on an examining table. I would take Little Rubes to the clinic, and they'd let him play there, or sleep. I got a lot of sympathy as a single father.

At the same time I would be on call for an orthopedic doctor. I told him my situation and said, "Here's the deal. Schedule all your X-rays from like eleven o'clock to one o'clock, five or six patients, and pay me seventy-five or a hundred dollars per patient." This arrangement was fine with him because he was just grateful to have somebody to take his X-rays. Then when I took a lunch break from the clinic, I would do the orthopedic doctor's patients on my lunch hour.

What's strange is that it took me a long time to get over the feeling that there was something wrong with this, like I was stealing the money. I mean, nobody I knew had ever made this kind of money—not legally. So I felt that at some point someone would tell me that I couldn't do it anymore. I actually felt guilty.

I was just a hyper person, but I don't know if I could do it anymore. I would sleep like two days to get over the round-the-clock shifts. When I look back, I was beating myself up. After a few years of this, though, I was able to buy a home in the Pico area for my father and at almost the same time buy a house for me and Al. Housing prices weren't anything like what they are now, and my father sold the house on Ulysses, and Al helped out, so it was easy. I actually owned three or four homes in that area over the years—housing prices were still pretty low.

I was making an incredible amount of money as far as I was concerned, I didn't have debts, and I had more money than I knew what to do with. I wasn't saving up for anything, but it wasn't really about getting rich either. And the police were still stopping me, shaking me down, looking for anything they could bust me on. Eventually they did bust me, and once again I was behind bars for some kind of probation violation or other, something minor. What was strange was that this time, jail really did change my life, if not the way the system expected it to.

5

The Greatest Motorcycle Club in the World

had never been into motorcycles. Nobody thinks about motorcycles growing up in a Hispanic neighborhood. It was always cars. The only motorcycle club you used to hear about then was the Hells Angels, and they were a white club, mostly, so nobody thought about joining them or thought much about motorcycles at all. But in jail that last time, my cellmate had *Easy Rider* magazines, and he left them lying around. You have a lot of time in jail, you know, so I picked up a copy, and I saw a picture of a Harley, all fixed up and chromed. I thought, *Firme.*

That was the beginning. I started collecting magazines and pictures in there. Somebody would bring them there, and I would end up with them. I think at that point, I was completely away from the drive-by gang mentality. I think I was just getting tired of it. I was in my early thirties, and I had gotten to a point where something inside was saying that it was time to stop. I don't know if it's because my body couldn't take it anymore or my mind didn't want to do it anymore. Or a little of both.

I think what I saw in motorcycles was a way of still being somewhat wild, of allowing that renegade side of myself to come out. I'm sure at the back of my mind I was thinking I could stay out of the mess and still live a little on the wild side. I'd never ridden a motorcycle before, but I started reading up on them, and I decided that when I got out I was going to look into that scene.

When I was released, a couple of old friends came to pick me up, and they asked me what I wanted to do. I said that I wanted to look at motorcycles, and they looked at me like I had lost my mind. That's the way it was for a while. I would talk to other people about motorcycles, but it was like talking to them about submarines. But when I've decided something, it's pretty hard to stop me. The next free afternoon I had, between looking for jobs and trying to get my life back together, I walked into the nearest Harley-Davidson dealer I could find, over in Fullerton.

The bike that looked really outstanding to me was a wide 1982 Shovelhead FLH, a genuine hog, factory red with a big front fender and cowl headlight. It was in really good shape for a used bike. As far as I was concerned, it was the most beautiful bike I'd ever seen, better even than the ones in the magazines. I told the salesperson I wanted it and put a few bucks down to hold it. The guy agreed—not forever, he said, but for a little while. I put together the rest of the money, legally. I was working again, and Al could help, and so on. I was afraid someone else might buy the bike if I didn't come up with the money quick enough. The next thing I knew I had a pink slip that meant I owned a Harley.

That is, I had a Harley I didn't know how to ride. I asked around and found someone who worked with my brother, Al, a guy named Pete Cano. I got him on the phone, explained my situation to him, and he agreed to meet me at the showroom and drive my bike out of there. I followed him home in a car and I watched my bike going down the freeway. I thought it was beautiful.

Pete helped me out in the beginning, taught me about compression ratios and stuff like that and how to shift the gears, turn, and the rest. I would take it out and just ride down my street in Pico, at like five miles per hour. I would turn around in the driveways. I did that for days up and down my street, into driveways, back and forth, to the corner, little by little. People would come out and admire the bike. I mean, everybody's impressed by a Harley. The next thing you know, I was going around the block. One day I knew I couldn't wait anymore and I took the ramp up to the freeway and opened it up.

That was a wonderful moment for me, and it made me sure I had made the right choice. I took it up to sixty-five, and the feeling that came over me was incredible, the wind whipping past me, and me whipping past cars. It really is a feeling of freedom you can't have any other way.

I remember taking it to the DMV in Montebello to take the road test, and the guy said, "Do you really want to take the test on that? Not too many people pass it on this bike. They usually rent or borrow smaller bikes." I said, "Look, this is what I'm going to ride every day. I'll take it on this." He just shrugged and said okay. When I passed the test, he actually complimented me; he said that usually only chippies—the California Highway Patrolmen—passed on a bike that big.

So now I could ride, but I was just riding around by myself. None of my buddies had bikes, so it wasn't like I could go to my neighborhood to get a group together and have a run. They didn't have the money and they weren't interested; it wasn't a thing Hispanics did.

But I did go around to the bike shows and bike runs and events like that, and I started meeting a lot of people.

I had met a lot of them before in my gangbanging days. I knew them but they were from different areas, so there was no trouble between us. Every once in a while I would see a group from Whittier, or Highland Park, or I would run into a group from the San Fernando Valley and we would talk. They weren't a club, it was just two or three friends riding around. And it was always Harleys; Harleys had that hard-core appeal to them. It's interesting that all these ex-gangbangers and hard-core street people were getting into bikes about the same time. People in my situation, people who wanted to put some distance between themselves and the gangs, but they still had that wild hair up their ass.

Another thing I noticed at these bike runs was that the Hells Angels or the Vagos had this attitude, like, "Well, there are fifty of us or a hundred of us, so don't get in our way." It was like being in junior high again. I would think, *Who are you? Who are you to cut in line in front of me?* And I thought, *This is bullshit, this is just not going to happen.* I'm nobody to disrespect.

About that time I discovered the Mongols. There would be a hundred Angels, or fifty Vagos, but you would only see like seven Mongols. Yet nobody ever messed with them; they were really respected. That impressed me. After all, I had been through quite a bit. I decided to find out more about them.

I had heard some rumors about the club. The Mongols had been founded in 1970 in East L.A., Montebello to be exact, by a couple of Harley riders who liked to ride, party, and fight. The first national president of the Mongols was a fellow by the name of Louis Costello, who'd named his club after Genghis Khan, the great Mongol conqueror of Asia. The Mongols had been popular early on, but lately, for one reason or another, the club hadn't been very visible.

Almost all the early members were Mexican, with maybe one or two white guys, like this guy Dick I got to know at the meets, who was still a Mongol and who ran a motorcycle shop in East L.A.

The first generation of Mongols was fiercely loyal. Six of the charter members lived on the same street in El Sereno. In their heyday the Mongols had been a feared organization filled with dangerous men who didn't take shit from no one. They could be mean when they drank, and they drank all the time, but they also drove the best bikes around. Eventually the club began to expand. They added chapters in Los Angeles, San Diego, and central California. They even reached as far as Oklahoma. The Mongols attracted an interesting bunch of tough guys, including one Navy veteran, an ex-SEAL who would one day go on to become the governor of Minnesota. His name is Jesse Ventura. We called him "Superman."

By the mid-1970s the old guard had been replaced by newer members, and the next national president of the club was a fellow by the name of Andy Holguin, called Maravilla, which is Spanish for "wonderful" or "marvelous." Maravilla was interested in expanding the club's reach within California and set his sites on the San Fernando Valley, just over the hill from Los Angeles proper.

The only problem was that that turf was already taken by a small but tough outlaw club called Satan's Slaves. When the Mongols first showed up in the valley, they were told by the Slaves to get out, to which the Mongols replied, "Fuck your mother." The Mongols thought that was going to be the end of it, but the problem was, the Satans had the same answer for us. But then, Satan's Slaves disappeared. The Satans had gone to another club for help, and the price they had to pay was to be swallowed whole.

As a result, the Mongols were no longer up against a small, proud group but a much larger one named the Hells Angels. Ever since the 1960s, the Hells Angels had "owned" California and had beaten back any challenge to that. They claimed their ownership with a patch that said CALIFORNIA, which curved up like the foot of a rocking chair under their main patch, the death's head. Everybody called that the California rocker. They demanded that every other club use only their city on a rocker. No one except the Hells Angels, as far as they were concerned, had the right or the balls to fly California. The Mongols disagreed. They started flying the California rocker under their Mongol rider patch. Naturally, the Angels didn't like this and wouldn't give in without fighting.

At a bike show at the *Queen Mary,* docked in San Diego, the president of the Hells Angels' San Bernardino chapter was killed. The Mongols had showed up there but were leaving, and the Hells Angels followed them to the parking lot. All hell broke loose, and the Hells Angels chapter president ended up getting stabbed to death. Then a Hells Angel in San Diego was killed. In 1987 two Mongols, Red Beard and Jingles, were heading home from a bike run, riding down Interstate 15 with their women on the backs of their bikes. A van pulled up alongside. Someone opened a window in the van, stuck a submachine gun through it, and blew them all to kingdom come.

For a while, explosives were used freely. During one of our funerals, somebody parked a car in front of the funeral home and it blew up. They blew up a shop in Highland Park by putting dynamite into a motorcycle tire. They brought the bike to the shop and said they wanted the flat fixed. It blew up and killed the kid brother of a Mongol. He worked at the shop, but he wasn't even a Mongol. The Mongols had no intention of giving in to them or anyone else, no matter how many bullets they shot at us. The Mongols would defend themselves, no matter how many died.

As in all other wars, sooner or later an agreement was reached. The war with the Hells Angels eventually fizzled out—the two groups had a meeting and agreed to peace. The Mongols became the first club other than the Hells Angels to wear California, and we're still the only club ever to earn that right.

I started hanging around with the Mongols, and I would go on the runs with them and talk to people about them. I've always been able to talk to people.

Then one weekend, there was going to be a national run, an event the whole club would join in. I was psyched for the ride. It was a beautiful day. The only problem was, the run was held in an open field, nothing there—no music, no band, nothing, not even an outhouse. It was one of the most boring things you can imagine. And only about twenty Mongols showed up, and none of them were on the near side of thirty. That day I was talking with Junior, the national president of the club—always called "the pres"—who was a white guy about five-foot-five and covered with tattoos. I asked him why the rest of the members didn't come. "Hey, man," he said, "that's what we're down to."

I took a deep breath as I stood among the other Harleys. I just couldn't believe it. This was a club that had had, at one time, more than a hundred members with a strong and tough reputation. I asked him why they didn't go on a run that was more exciting, where something is happening and people are there. I couldn't believe what he told me. Because the membership was down, he said, he had put out the word that Mongols should never be seen together in public as a group because then everyone would know how few there were.

He then introduced me to the club's national vice president, Long-haired Dave (David Rivera), who seemed nice enough but in my opinion not exactly what I'd call leadership material. I talked to some of the other members for a while, and as we talked, and as I watched them there and later, I found out some interesting things. They had so few members not just because of the violence or advancing age. In fact, a lot of former Mongols had given up on the club because the leadership was fucked up. Their mentality was totally wrong. It was not just "us against them," it was "the rest of the world is guilty until proven innocent." For instance, their idea of how to treat new members was this: If you came around, they would beat you up. If you came back, they would beat you up again. If you came back after that, then you could stay. What kind of self-respecting guy was going to put up with that shit? They were fortunate that they hadn't tried to beat me up; there would have been even fewer members.

But even once they accepted you, you started out as a prospect, meaning you had to do whatever they told you to do for about a year. Some prospects were actually abused—a member could kick a prospect or slap one around. I remember there used to be the prospect Olympics, where they would get four or five prospects and drink until two in the morning and then make them race one another and climb trees—just do weird shit. Somebody told me there used to be marshmallow races. They would make the prospects put a marshmallow in the crack of their ass and then race from one end of a field to the other. The loser had to eat all the marshmallows. This didn't happen every time, with every chapter, but there were cases. They'd make you kneel on top of your bike frame and grab it while they swatted you with a huge paddle until your ass bled; you couldn't move or you'd get beat up even more. How do you bring in a guy who ran the program at the state prison when members indulge in this kind of stupidity?

There were some pretty standard things. There was a fee of say a hundred and thirty dollars for investigations. This was supposedly for the costs of finding out who you were and if you were good enough to join the Mongols, but I found out later there was more.

As with most clubs at the time, you were supposed to give them the pink slip for your motorcycle.

That wasn't as crazy as it sounds, in a way. You have to remember that the police thought that all the motorcycle clubs—at least the Hells Angels and the Mongols and some of the others—were just criminal organizations. They still think so. But anyway, the police were always trying to get members to become snitches. These were guys who carried weapons and were ignorant of the laws and did drugs, so they were always getting busted for something or other, even if they weren't hurting anybody but themselves. So the police would bust a member and threaten him with hard jail time unless he agreed to inform on the club. But since the club was holding the pink slip to a guy's bike, the club still had some leverage. They also held the slip to keep you from quitting. They were so short of members that the club had a rule that you had to bring in two members a year or you were fined five hundred dollars.

Another thing I noticed about the club in those early days was that there were never any women around. Or at least any women you might want to have around. But once I spent a little time with the members at some parties, I could see why—they totally disrespected women. They would hit women. If a woman talked back to one of the Mongols it would be an automatic back of the hand to her. They treated women like shit and even sometimes slapped them around for no reason—in other words, it was really bullshit. That was manly to them, but the way I looked at it was totally the opposite; there is nothing manly about that. If you want to be a man, give a Hells Angel the back of your hand.

The more I learned about the club, the more I thought, *This is ridiculous.* But at the same time, I knew the reputation was there.

The name Mongols is wonderful, the patch is wonderful, the idea of a Mongol, in history, is wonderful. Those guys rode around and conquered everything in sight. I think that's a very powerful image for the people in the club. The Mongols weren't afraid of anyone. The club already had Hispanics in it, so they wouldn't keep us out for that. It was perfect. This was an organization I could take and turn into something. I wanted the club to grow and I thought I could do it.

Now some people thought, and probably still think, that this was all a power trip for me. But it was never really about power—I had never run any organization, never been in charge of anything but myself and Little Rubes. I just saw the club as being something that everyone could benefit from.

I know this will sound crazy, but believe it or not I was looking ahead to when we would have a lot of members, and I thought about it like a business, with the members like the employees. Now what do employees want? They want security and they want benefits. So I thought about getting together as a group to buy medical insurance—of course, that would be a tough one. One of the things that I envisioned was to have so many members that we could actually get a business license and sell wholesale. I wanted to have a clubhouse and more than a clubhouse, a clubhouse that was also part Wal-Mart. I wanted to be able to purchase in bulk—milk or motor oil, whatever we needed. I wanted to open up a motorcycle shop where we could buy parts at cost and sell them at just enough of a profit to pay the overhead. We could have an accountant do the books so that we didn't get screwed. I wanted my club not only to be great and big, but I wanted to make it easier for the members financially. In other words, I wanted this to be a huge organization.

I had a meeting with Junior in the backyard of a home in Pico Rivera and I told him that I wanted to come in, I wanted to prospect, or whatever was necessary. He said, "Instead of prospecting in an existing chapter, why don't you start a chapter and run it yourself?" He was basically making me a chapter president without ever having been a regular member. This had never been done before. Normally it takes forever to work your way up to being a chapter president. I thought at the time that they appreciated that I was a serious person and had a background and they liked that. I would learn many things in those first years with the club.

I had already talked to some people who would be good members, good for the club, and they had agreed to come in. One was Joe "Apeman" Mendez, who was about fifty-five years old, owned his own tire shop, and had been riding forever. He'd never been a member of a club; he just loved riding his bike. There was Pony (Guillermo Lara), who was a young guy with a ponytail and a lot of tattoos, two kids and a wife, no gang background. The third was Largo, six-foot-one, heavily bearded, big mustache, owned a wrought-iron company. And the fourth was Money (Martin Guevara), a clean-cut guy with a city job I'd known from when I was a kid; he was the one who introduced me to the others. None of these guys had to prospect. They didn't have to prove anything to me.

But then I went around to all the different neighborhoods and saw all the people I had known either from being locked up or just from being on the streets, and there were a lot of guys who all had Harleys. I decided to have a meeting at my house and explain what I was thinking, so I let them all know. Well, there were so many people that they wouldn't all fit in my house at the same time.

I had to set up meetings on two different nights, about eighty to ninety people each night. Most of them were ex–gang members or people who lived in gang-infested areas who had wanted to migrate away from actual gang life, like me. They came to my house with their flannels, their Dickies jackets, their bald heads, parking their motorcycles outside. Not everyone there was an ex-gangbanger—there were some longhair bikers, but none of them belonged to a group. The room was full and they were pouring out into the yard. You can imagine what the neighbors thought about eighty Harleys parked along the street.

So I got up in front of everybody and told them what I was thinking about. I simply told them that if we joined, we could run our own program and we could add a lot to the club. There are things that I don't like about the Mongols right now, I said, but we could change them if we became strong enough.

They had a lot of questions. The club had a solid reputation as far as defending itself, but everybody knew about how the Mongols beat up the public. There were a lot of other stories going around about the club, some of which were true and some not. One was that the Mongols had a right to some of your paycheck. Another was that they had a right to your wife whenever they wanted her. All this stuff sounds crazy now, but you have to remember that at the time it was a top-secret organization. Nobody even knew how many members there were. There were a lot of shot-callers from various neighborhoods at the meeting, people who had reputations and were not about to be slapped around.

The rumor about the pink slip was true, and a lot of these guys wouldn't sign on to that. They were men of their word. They didn't want to sign on to anything and then have to go back on it. I told them if we all got into this we could run our own program. I told them the way I thought the club could go: We would do our thing together, we would be there for one another. I said that the club could be a brotherhood, a place where everybody looked out for one another.

When those meeting were over, no one had volunteered to join except the original four, because the Mongols had such a bad reputation. In fact, the phone didn't ring for a week, but I wasn't worried, because I knew that I could get things done. I didn't know how many would come or when, but I knew that they would come eventually. A week later I went to Junior with Apeman, Largo, Pony, and Money and said, "I got my guys. I want to start my chapter." There wasn't a big ceremony with the club when we got our colors, but it was a big moment for us. We shook hands and we hugged and I think there was a bond between us five from that moment on.

Right after that, we went to a Harley run in Palm Springs. I had to ask permission to bring my chapter, because they still didn't want too many members together in a crowded place. "How are you ever going to grow if you're being so secretive?" I asked. "How are people going to see you and say, 'Hey, I like that group—I want to join'?" Finally they agreed. So we went and we were very proud to go as a chapter for the first time, the Mongols Pico chapter. And we were visible. I remember sitting at a club called Chillers with the other four, all wearing our colors, and people started approaching us, saying things like, "Hey Doc, we heard you did this and we're interested. There are some things that we got to work out but we like the idea."

A lot of people asked if I could guarantee that they would be with me and not the old Mongols. I told them I could guarantee it because I had been promised that I could have that chapter. Whether Junior or Long-haired Dave or Red Dog meant to keep that promise or not didn't matter to me, because I wasn't going to let them take it away from me.

People must have liked what they saw, because I was approached by numerous individuals that whole weekend. I think right there I must have picked up about another fifteen or twenty people. They were mostly Hispanic, along with one Hawaiian guy and one or two white guys. Those who didn't know me asked questions, and I guess they got positive answers because I started getting lots of phone calls after Palm Springs. I didn't automatically say yes to everyone, but I could tell that people really wanted to believe that this could happen. They wanted to wear the Mongol patch. I had to take their money for the investigation fee and say we would get back to them, but I actually did all the investigation that was necessary.

The next chapter to start up after Pico was El Sereno, and they started it up on their own. Two guys named Lucifer and Buggs knew a bunch of guys who hung out in El Sereno. They had a meeting and called me up to ask if it were possible to start a chapter "because there are quite a few of us here." I thought it was great, and I said I would try to work something out. But of course that meant I had to deal with Junior and see if he was interested in letting that happen.

But the Mongol reputation was still causing me problems. While I was waiting for Junior to make a decision, the El Sereno chapter just kind of disintegrated. Only two guys said they were willing to commit, because the others had started to hear all the rumors and nonsense about the club. So with only two, Lucifer and Buggs, there weren't enough to start a chapter, but I could bring them into Pico by myself. And they came into Pico, I gave them their patches, and in like two hours Lucifer and Buggs started to get calls on their cell phones, and all the rest of their guys committed. So I said that maybe they could create El Sereno, since Pico would have been too big with all those new members.

But that made another problem because in the old days they had a rule that you had to stay in a chapter for a year or two. It amazes me that in the old days everything was about forcing you to do things. Why would you need to force somebody if it wasn't a fucked-up place to be? Obviously I didn't play that game, but I also wanted to stick by the rules.

There were rules about investigating people because the Hells Angels and some of the other clubs had those rules, but the people

I was bringing in were different. The Hells Angels were bringing in people they didn't know in the community and so they couldn't follow up on them. But the Hispanics I was meeting had roots—or a tail, to put it another way—in the neighborhood. If you're a Hispanic out of East L.A. or any other Hispanic area, I can go back and do my homework on you. It's very simple. More than likely you grew up in a neighborhood where there was a gang. Either you were in the gang or the gang would know your name and your reputation. If a guy from the Avenues wanted to come in, all I needed to do was go down to his neighborhood and ask around about him. If a person came from an old rival of the Avenues I would not turn him away. We were supposed to be leaving that behind.

For the same reason, I didn't ask for these guys to prospect. The other clubs had to make new members jump through hoops, but if a guy just finished eight or ten years at Folsom Prison or Pelican Bay and he stood his ground there and maybe even ran the program, I didn't have to worry that he had what I was looking for. Am I going to be saying to him, "Hey, go get me a beer, you flunky"? It's not going to happen. And there is no need for it. I relaxed a lot of those rules and that helped us grow, although some people criticized me for it.

Another criticism was that we weren't bikers because we didn't have long blond hair, and because we showered, and because we didn't use meth. A lot of our guys have shaved heads and they're very neat about the creases in their pants and things like that. I don't think you have to smell bad to be a biker, and I don't think the color or length of your hair makes a difference.

On the opposite side of the coin, when we first hit the culture people said, "They're not bikers, they're gangbangers," because they were seeing Hispanics with shaved heads. But I let all the new members know that we were not a gang. We were not in existence to hurt anyone who hadn't hurt us. We were not in existence to make connections for crime or for drugs. It's just a different kind of prejudice to keep somebody out of the club because he used to gangbang. I did too. The bottom line is if you were no longer into gangbanging and you were into riding a motorcycle, then you could be a biker with the Mongols.

During my first year in the club, I brought in about two hundred new members. That was the problem.

6

Old Dogs

was so busy bringing new members in and figuring out ways to start new chapters so that I could bring in even more new members that I didn't always think about what was happening behind my back. I had made the club ten times bigger, but not everybody thought the club was ten times better. The people who were digging in their heels the deepest were, naturally, the old-timers, and especially the leaders of the club—Junior, Long-haired Dave, and Red Dog.

I always thought Junior wasn't too bad. He was a short guy, a white guy with blond hair, and I always thought he had balls. But let's face it, the club was down to almost nothing while he was in charge, and there were all these moronic attitudes and habits. He may have been an OK guy, but anyone could see that he was not a very good national president.

Then there was Long-haired Dave, who was the national vice president. He was OK as a person, but not very aggressive. For example, Dave worked at Bartell's Harley-Davidson, which is the center of the Harley universe, and people from other clubs used to go there and yell at him and put him down when he was at work. Other people who worked there would call us up to let us know about this, and we would zoom in from wherever we were to make sure nothing happened to one of our national officers. When we asked him why he let those guys treat him that way, he would say, "Well, I know the guys. I've known them for a long time."

That may very well be, but when our whole world is about respect, we couldn't have people beating up on a national officer. Once when I was heading down there to bail him out, I ran into a hardware store and bought several ball-peen hammers. I was ready to break a few fingers. I would have taken whatever punishment Dave was going to deal out for doing that, but I was going to put an end to them shaking their fingers in his face. Well, once I showed up with those hammers, the guys from the other clubs just got on their bikes and they were gone. And of course Dave never did anything to me.

The national president gets to choose the other national officers; Junior and Red Dog later told me that they had picked Dave for vice president because they knew he was no threat to them and because Dave was Hispanic, which covered them with the majority of the members on that count.

Then there was Red Dog, and he was a piece of work. He had spiderwebs tattooed on the outside corner of his eyes and a huge swastika on his belly. He always wore a leather trench coat, like a Nazi. Red Dog and Junior had a lot of things in common. They both loved to wear a lot of gold—big gold chains and big gold rings. They were both heavily into meth, and neither of them had a job. These were the guys who ran the mother chapter, which is known as the Southern California chapter. It's the only chapter that's not based in a city. But Red Dog hung out a lot with the San Fernando Valley chapter—mainly, I think, because all those guys were idiots. That was the chapter that Billy Queen infiltrated. Junior and Red Dog had gained control of the club because the majority of the guys left in the club were like them. They were more into shoving stuff up their noses than defending anything. My crowd were hardened *soldados*.

At first they were all really happy that I was bringing in all these members. After all, there was the investigation fee, and I guess they were making about a hundred and forty dollars' profit off the patches and other paraphernalia they sold to the new members. So they were loving it, plus they loved the fact that if any of those guys stepped out of line they figured they were going to take his bike. Red Dog once told me later that the only reason they let me bring in all those people is because they thought they wouldn't last.

They not only took motorcycles from prospects they threw out, but they took just about everything else. They forced people out of the club so they could take all of their stuff. They would rent a U-Haul truck and go to their homes when the ex-member wasn't there and take anything portable—toasters, a typewriter, a stereo, a television, anything. Because they were tweakers—junkies. A tweaker will grab a toaster oven and ask for five bucks for it on the street. That was when meth was really cheap. I don't know exactly how much it cost because I haven't done drugs since I started with the Mongols. I'm against drugs because they make an army weak. I remember one time going to Red Dog's and it was full of briefcases, typewriters, and the other little petty shit that a tweaker sells.

Nobody fought back because they were afraid—the Mongol reputation was a powerful thing. I knew the stealing was going on. I was never invited in on it and I'm glad of that, but I knew they were going in and taking shit. I stuck to my program—build up the club and I could do things my way eventually. And that's how it worked out. Red Dog's greediness was eventually his downfall.

Greed made them let new members in, but their fear of doing anything different made them slow down the process to a crawl. One of the hardest things for a man to face is that what he's doing isn't working and he has to change. (I say a man, but of course I mean anyone. In the club it's always men.) Anyway, it was easier for them to keep doing things the way they had been doing, to lay low and beat up on civilians, than to become something bigger and better and run the risks that involves. I would find out more about the risks later—not that knowing sooner would have stopped me.

From the beginning, a lot of people I knew said that the old guard was going to try and pull a fast one on me. They had a lot of little tricks. Say if three people wanted to start a chapter, they would say fine, come on in. But once the new members had started their chapter, Junior or Red Dog would suddenly complain that things weren't being run right and they would install another president, one of their people, in the chapter. Then they'd find a way to squeeze the new guys. It was a bait-and-switch thing. They were really well known for that.

But not everyone in the club was a bad guy. One of my best friends and a real ally was a guy nicknamed JC, who came into the club just after I did. He was a big help during this time. JC was a big man with long white hair and he was the kind of person who could dominate a room whenever he walked into it. He was very persuasive—you just couldn't say no to JC unless you were a total knucklehead. He had always had problems with the way some of the things happened in the club, but he really loved it and wanted to make it better.

Monster was another one. Monster is a very big guy, mean looking and a good fighter too. Monster's father was a well-known boxer around here in Los Angeles, and he brought up his kids to box, so Monster can defend himself. When he first came in we had trouble collecting dues from him and things like that, but he would always show up to help when there was trouble and he could really liven up a party. He has a serious sense of humor. He can make you laugh forever. We would sit in church—the meeting at the mother chapter—and he would have us rolling with his jokes.

One time when Monster was prospecting the club was getting ready for a run, and this old-timer, a real bully called Craze, came up and offered to shake Monster's hand. Monster put his hand out and the guy grabs Monster's thumb and just twists it. Because Monster was prospecting, he had to take whatever was dished out to him. So this old guy is torturing Monster to see how much pain Monster could handle. Monster started to sweat—not because of the pain he was feeling, but from the anger. This was an example of how the old guard treated members.

I walked up because I could see something was wrong, and the guy let go and walked away. Monster was about to explode, so I called over the secretary of the treasury of my chapter at the time, Money. I told him to go get a top rocker for Monster. Once you get your top rocker, you're a fully pledged member, which means you're equal to anyone in the club. I told Money to give the rocker to Monster and get it sewed on really quick. Monster came back in about two minutes with his top rocker, and I just said, "Go get him." Monster took off like a bat out of hell. This was maybe seven years ago, and I haven't seen Craze since. That was Monster's ceremony.

There were some great parties there, good times too. We changed the idea of what a Mongol run should be. Not only were we visible, we were visibly having a great time. When the whole club went on a run, each chapter would kind of pick out a spot where that chapter would congregate. I mean you went all around, everyone was a brother, but you also had a home base where your chapter would be. Our spot, the Pico spot, and some of the other spots of chapters I'd started, they were rocking. We had music, we had good-looking women, we had lights, we had chairs, we had food and drinks, we had everything you needed. If there was something we wanted to bring, we brought it. We were getting to a point where people were starting to think, *What are we going to do now to top that?*

We got a lot of smirks about our chapter because of all those comforts we packed onto the bikes. The older guys thought it wasn't manly or something. In fact, I remember one time hearing comments about being the Barbie chapter. But nobody could really say that—or get away with saying it, either—because we were hardcore. We would later be called the wrecking crew because we would handle all the business that the club needed done. So nobody was eager to offend us.

But I made sure that the parties didn't degenerate into the kind of stupidity that the old Mongols were known for. I had to lay down some rules of my own, and I made sure that they were enforced. I wouldn't allow any fights with civilians and wouldn't allow any disrespect of women. No one could ask a prospect to do anything that the member himself wouldn't do. No one was allowed to hit on another Mongol's woman, which is a rule that almost all the clubs enforce anyway.

So it evolved from sitting around in a tent looking at one another. After the Pico chapter had been together for about a year, we decided to have an anniversary party. Of course an anniversary party would be a run, and I thought we should go back to Palm Springs, where the chapter really started to attract attention that first year. At the same time, we knew that the old guard was looking for any little reason to get rid of me, so I figured that if anything happened to one of the guys there, getting drunk or arrested, they would use that as an excuse to toss me out. But I also wanted to have that run there because I wanted to recruit.

We decided to have the run at a hotel, for the first time in the history of the Mongols—and for the first time we were going to show our strength to the public. We found a small hotel on the outskirts of Palm Springs that had separate little houses around the swimming pool. Each chapter had its own bungalow. The deal was that if you got drunk, you'd stay in your chapter room. If you didn't feel like you could drive home, you could stay in your chapter room until you did. We would pay for all of it, out of the dues from the chapter. For the whole year our chapter had put aside extra money. Every member put in a little bit every month. We saved enough so we could rent the whole little hotel plus hire a band. To complete the picture, we had a pool table shipped there and placed by the side of the swimming pool. We brought in all the food and all the liquor that anyone could want. That way, no one had to go around the town and maybe get involved in an altercation with the civilians, or crash a bike or anything like that. It was a huge success. Everybody who came had a terrific time.

Still, a lot of the old-time members actually boycotted Palm Springs. It's not surprising, I guess, that I constantly had serious arguments with all the national officers at the mother chapter, almost from the beginning. So did JC. I remember thinking about everything JC was doing for the club, how incredibly hard he was working, but all those guys did was get him into trouble. I'm a pretty good judge of character and pretty fair, but I just didn't like anything about them—Junior and Red Dog and some of the others, the ones who were really just bullies. Deep down I didn't like the kind of person they were.

As a result, I never really told them everything I wanted to do, what my long-range plan was. It wasn't even a plan exactly, and I'm sure my ideas would have sounded far-fetched to anybody but me. But I wasn't even pushing for the big plans yet, just for everyone to be treated fairly and consistently.

We argued about all kinds of things, because they were always trying to pull some piece of nonsense on us. I remember one time they tried to tell JC and me that they should get their way because they were senior members. There is no such thing as a senior member, there are no ranks based on how long you've been in the club. To have Junior or Red Dog call themselves senior members when we knew there was no such thing was a kind of disrespect. *What a crock of shit,* I thought to myself. I tried to speak out at meetings at the mother chapter whenever I could. Some of the original chapter presidents would pass me notes about questions I should ask, because they didn't want Junior to get on their case. I didn't give a fuck whether he liked the question or not, and I would ask it.

Junior and Red Dog were always trying to hammer the new guys, trying to catch them doing something wrong so that they could bust them back to prospecting and maybe make them want to quit. They tried to get just about everyone I had brought into the club. They would call them into church and yell at them, so JC and I decided we would defend the new guys. We started to act like their unofficial attorneys. We would find out the facts ahead of time and argue their case in the meeting. And it was usually a bullshit thing and Junior would have to back off.

We were spoiling their fun, so then they made up a rule that JC and I couldn't be in mother church together. And another rule was that when one of us was in church he would have to do his business and leave. They were basically setting it up so that they could convict the new guys without a legitimate argument or a decent defense. But the mother chapter should be open to everyone because that was our government. It's like your city council saying that a certain segment of the community can't come to its meetings but everyone else could. I was sort of proud of that rule, in a perverse way, because it showed that we were succeeding in defending the new guys. But they were trying to slow everything down, they just dragged their heels in every way possible. They even invented what they called slow-growth periods to stop me. They wouldn't allow any new members in for, say, three months.

I would come to Red Dog with a new member's application and the money for the investigation, and he would just say, "Give it to me," and stuff it in his pocket. Sometimes he would scribble something on the back of a Jack in the Box receipt, like he was making a note to himself about it, but I knew what was going on. A few weeks down the road he would ask me for the investigation money and I would say that I'd given it to him and he would say he didn't remember. Things like that started to happen too often. There were times when I paid the money myself. Meanwhile, Red Dog was not working and neither was Junior, yet both of them were surviving, they both had motorcycles, and Red Dog was still sticking stuff up his nose.

Also, Red Dog started to add more people to the club, especially in the San Fernando Valley chapter. He was trying to bring in more people who would support him, but most of these people were not really Mongols. That was one reason why Billy Queen became a Mongol. Even though Red Dog was suspicious of Billy, he let him join and pay his dues.

These guys found it so threatening that an outsider had come in and was trying to turn the club into a powerhouse all by himself that things started to get ugly. Junior and Red called me to a meeting with them one time. Red Dog said, "You know, Doc, Junior and I were playing the 'what-if' game." So I asked what that was, and Red Dog said, "Well, it's real simple. We were saying, 'What if Doc tried to take over the club?'"

I could see where this was heading, but in fact I didn't want to take over the club. "How could I do that?" I said. "There's the five-year rule. I will always abide by the rules that have been laid down." They had established a rule that no one could become a national officer until he had been in the club for five years. I really did want to follow all the rules. I wanted the club to be run correctly, so I wasn't going to go against any of the rules. "Besides," I said, "I don't want to take over the club. The members will vote, and why should they vote for someone who is so new to the club?"

"That's right, Doc," Red Dog said. "I'm glad to hear it, because otherwise there could be a problem." I didn't really think this tweaker was going to be able to cause me any problems personally, but what he was saying is they didn't want me to try to run for anything. That was OK with me. I was already so busy working on building the club that I had quit some of my extra radiology jobs. I worked the night shift at the hospital so that I could spend more time on the club.

Red Dog was still seeing dollar signs, not a strong club. He was so blinded by the money that he didn't realize it was already getting to be too late for him to do anything about it. But I think there are a lot of things he didn't see. I didn't mind him getting high, but it did bother me that he was getting other people hooked too. A lot of the members were shoving that crap up their nose, and it started to cause me problems. A couple of those older guys owned their own tattoo parlors, and my guys wanted to hang out with them and hear stories. Unfortunately, the only thing they were really getting was a habit. Monster and a lot of my other guys got hooked on meth because of them. I would take two steps forward and they would take me back a step, and it got to a point where I had to bar my guys from going to those tattoo parlors or hanging out with the old guys.

Then the next thing was that they came to me talking about

giving the national officers a salary, which would come out of the membership dues. They said that all the clubs were paying their nationals, and they even let slip that I might get a paycheck. I could see that they were trying to bribe me, and the people I'd brought into the club, into going along with them. They were becoming worried, but at the same time they were trying to find a way to make the new situation work in their favor. That only shows what knuckleheads they were.

They knew me a little but not enough to know that when you grow up in a gang in East L.A., you can't be bought. And you don't con your friends into doing something for money. You act this way because it's the only way to survive. Those rules were so much a part of me that I didn't even have to think about it, but I also knew from my days in the gangs that this was going to have to be dealt with.

One of the key people I brought in was Hank Munoz, who is always known as Cuete, which means "firecracker" in Spanish but is also used as a slang word for a gun. He is an incredible guy, known throughout Southern California. What is remarkable about him is that there are so many sides to him. He is someone with the mind and the calmness of a Don Corleone and the balls of Scarface, if you don't mind me using movie characters to describe him. He is an extremely dangerous person, and he's got a great heart. But he also has good sense. If he has a problem with you, he will hear you out. He looks at all sides of a situation and makes a decision, very quickly if necessary, about what the right thing to do is. I was even surprised that he was interested, and that he had a bike already. *This guy doesn't need anything to make himself respected,* I thought. *Can he really be interested in us?* But he was. It even made me feel more encouraged about the possibilities of the club.

He had been a member of a gang in Montebello and had been in and out of jail. When he first came around and the older guys heard

I was bringing him on they knew he was a real threat. That was the difference between us. Their thinking was not about making the club strong, but whether they could control it. Junior and Red Dog didn't want him in. They started screaming and spewing rumors about him—that he wouldn't be loyal, that he was going to be nothing but problems. I saw the guy as a big plus and I wouldn't let up.

One day they said, "If he really wants to come in, have him come down and talk to us." The meeting was held at my house, and they came prepared. There was security in the front, armed, which Red Dog had set up. Red Dog and Junior were there with several other members, and all of them were holding guns. That's how powerful Cuete's reputation was.

No one had to tell him that there would be weapons. No one had to tell him that this bunch of guys didn't like him. But he strolled up my walk as if it was no big deal. He's about five-foot-eight and stocky, solidly built. I thought, *Look at this guy. Anybody else would be wondering if he was going to walk out of here on his own two legs or not.* He sat down with all those guys facing him. They asked him if he wanted to come in the club and he said he did. Then Red Dog started asking some ridiculous bullshit. "There are some people you know," Red Dog said, "that we would like to get hold of. We'd like for you to give them up." He meant set them up. Red Dog still doesn't understand the barrio mentality: We don't give people up, we don't snitch.

Cuete looked at him and said, "I don't fucking do that."

I'm thinking, *Holy shit, here's a guy who is in somebody else's living room, he's got all these guys sitting around him, he has to know that they are all packing, and he basically tells Red to fuck off.* I thought this guy was either suicidal or he had more balls than anyone I knew. And I was kind of embarrassed because Red Dog had asked him to do something so against everything we grew up on.

But Red didn't know what to say. He just stared at him. Cuete said he still wanted to be in the club, and Red Dog didn't dare say a goddamn word to him. So Cuete walked out and left us to make a decision. Before I said anything to the members, I caught up with Cuete before he drove away. I assured him that I would make every effort to get him into the Mongols despite what Red Dog had said, that he was the kind of member we wanted—someone who represented the future rather than the past.

He left and I went back inside to hear Red Dog say, "Fuck no, I don't want that guy in. He doesn't want to play our game."

"Would you trust a guy," I asked everybody in the room, "if he turned his back on his brothers right now, after five minutes? Would you trust a guy like that? I think he gave us the answer we would want to hear."

Red Dog and Junior didn't understand that. So their answer was no.

A little while later they put together a run at some park that was mostly swamp up in central California and I thought there was going to be a rebellion. The whole club was there, and it turned into a discussion about Cuete. The old guys didn't want to bring him in. Some of them could barely stand they were so loaded, but they were shopping all this garbage about him, and about the club not being run right. It was one of the first times I felt there might be some serious problems, because suddenly my chapter just closed ranks around me. They literally formed a circle to back me up. Remember, I knew them all; they were serious men. You did not want to get into an argument with them.

JC said to one of the older guys, "You know what? Look at that man. He's going to be your next national president." I asked everybody just to calm down. I didn't want to start a fight that would tear the club apart. But I didn't give up, either. The club started to grow and I got criticized, but you have to remember one thing: Whenever you lead something you will be criticized. Even the president of the United States is criticized for everything he does. You just have to accept the fact that it's going to happen, no matter what.

Things started to get tense when Junior was sent to prison. I don't remember what it was for anymore, except that it wasn't about Mongol business. But that started a real struggle. Though he was in prison, Junior was still officially the president, but Red Dog thought it was time for him to take over since Junior wasn't coming out anytime soon. According to club rules, as vice president, Long-haired Dave should have become the president, but Red Dog didn't give a damn about that. He knew Dave would roll over if he pushed hard enough.

I would get phone calls from Red Dog about how I should support him and let all my people know that I was supporting him. "Otherwise," he said, "there's going to be a problem." There was no question in my mind what he meant; he was going to start shooting. He was full of shit, but he was also stupid enough to put himself in real danger. I didn't think all that much of Dave, but because Red Dog was a mess, I threw my support to him as the lesser of two evils. Also, there weren't that many members I could really support who had five years in the club. I offered my support to Leonard "Lenny" Valles, who was president of the East L.A. chapter, but he didn't want to take his time away from his chapter. The guys I could support were a little more realistic about themselves and whether they really would want to run the club. The ones who think they can usually can't.

When it became clear that I wasn't going to support Red Dog, that just made him madder, and his threats became more frequent. It got so bad that I had the members of my chapter standing armed guard in my front yard. Red Dog called me once and said, "Mike

Munz is getting out of prison. I'm going to have Mike come and talk to you." I said that I had no problem with that, but I also asked around about this fellow. People said Mike was crazy, which is a kind of compliment in our world—it meant he was capable of doing anything. He was a white guy from San Diego who had done a lot of time. Mike's idea of fun was to walk into the prison yard and say, "I'm Mike Munz. If anyone has a problem with that, let's just get it over with now." This was Red Dog's attempt to intimidate me. Mike was supposed to come out of prison and deal with me. He was their secret weapon. Another thing Red Dog didn't understand was the kind of life I had lived in the barrio. He didn't realize that our way of thinking is *You can bleed like anybody else.*

When Mike first came around we were having a party at La Vida Hot Springs, which is a bar up in the mountains where we go pretty often. Monster was prospecting again, which he does a lot because he screws up so much. Prospecting can also be a kind of light punishment when you don't pay your dues or you step out of line somehow. Anyway, Mike came in and got on Monster's ass about something— nothing that was out of line, since Monster was prospecting, but I had been waiting for Mike. I walked up to him and said, "Hey, what's the problem?"

We both knew why he was there, so we walked behind a shack beside the bar to take care of business with each other. Mike started with me and we exchanged a few words, but then I realized that he really wasn't looking for trouble. What's even funnier is that Mike thought the same thing about me. The argument stopped before it started, and we kind of walked away from each other. Later on we even became friends. He was a white guy, but he had been through the same life as me. He had been behind bars and he knew what was going on and he wasn't afraid of me or anything else. And like me, he didn't go around beating people up unless they started a fight. I don't fear anybody, but I'm glad Mike was a levelheaded person.

In the meantime, the club was getting bigger, and now the old guys were having trouble slowing down the growth. They wanted to, but they knew that if they did, the people already in the club were going to ask what the hell was going on. The floodgates were open, and I was bringing in strong serious people who were taking my side. So basically the old-timers were fucked. The one thing they had left to stop progress was the five-year rule.

I would go to meetings where they would accuse me of something in the hopes of making me mad so that I would break one of their rules and they could throw me out without starting a rebellion. I covered my ass in every way possible. There was a guy, a major drug dealer, who was having an argument with the club. He and his crew had picked a fight with some Mongols, and he got his ass kicked and lost his Rolex. He was really steamed, so when I heard this I set up a meeting to find out what was up and how we could settle this without people getting killed. So I went to one of the national officers I knew, Bobby Loco, our national sarge at the time, and told him I was going to meet with the guy. Bobby said, "OK, give it a try."

But when the others found out about the meeting they said that I shouldn't be having meetings like this without permission from the top. They really thought they had me that time. They thought they could get the votes to throw me out of the club, and they were working at it so hard I began to wonder what I would do if they succeeded. I had never thought about starting my own club. I loved the patch so much. I thought that if they tried to take my colors, there would be two clubs, but they would be two Mongol clubs. One would be those old tweakers and the other would be my people. From the very beginning, when it started to snowball, I made up my mind I would never give up. They could have their own meetings with twenty guys and I would lead the rest of the Mongols. In a church meeting I told Red Dog, "If you ever want my colors, you know where I live. But don't be the first one down my walkway." I wouldn't have hesitated to fight it out with him, with any weapon I had.

So although I didn't think Dave would be strong enough to lead the new Mongols, he at least could be president. If he was really as weak as they thought, I would be able to do what I needed to do. But I learned an interesting thing when I talked to Dave about being president. He hadn't been in the club for five years. Dave told me not to worry, it wasn't a problem, because at the time they had yet another rule: If you were already a national officer you could run for any national office, no matter how long you had been in the club. This made it even more interesting that Junior and Red Dog knew Dave wasn't a strong person. He hadn't even been elected; they had just picked him. They could have picked Mike Munz, for instance, but they knew he would stand up to them.

When we held elections that summer, I stood up and said that I was voting for Dave and he was elected pretty easily. Red Dog was pissed, but there wasn't much he could do. I had too many members on my side, and they were members who would not stand for any nonsense. It must have pissed off Red Dog even more that he had lost to the person he had chosen to be a patsy. Red Dog eventually faded away. Besides, he wasn't going to be able to make as much money from the club as he used to. I thought it meant that the old-timers would see that there was a new Mongols club. What I didn't know was that Red Dog had already done more damage to the Mongols than I'd ever imagined.

7

Angels' Fall

ave's election made it pretty clear that I was a power broker in the club, but I was still more interested in making the club bigger than in holding the reins of power. I still feel that way, but one of the things I learned from working with Dave and with the next president is that power can be a very dangerous thing. I had always thought that Dave wasn't an aggressive person. That's what Red Dog had said, and that was pretty much what I had seen. At the time, I felt that his lack of aggressiveness would fit with my idea of where the club should go—or at least it wouldn't slow me down.

One of the first things I did when Dave became president was to try again to get Cuete in the club. He was still willing, and he had come around the club some more and eventually convinced people that he belonged. Cuete was admitted along with his homeboy Shorty

(Alex Alcantar), a young, tall, very likable individual who was also extremely dangerous. That was encouraging.

Red Dog and Junior had fought me about opening new chapters and making the club bigger. I figured that Dave didn't have enough balls to fight about anything. He would just take advantage of the perks of being president—mainly that people pay you some respect and buy you drinks and it's probably easier to pick up girls—and let me go on with bringing in new members and starting new chapters. After a couple of years in the club, I thought it was pretty clear what I was trying to do; it was obvious I wanted to grow the club, and it was obvious that Dave was the president only because I had provided him with the votes. But once he was elected, he started making decisions on his own, without consulting the membership. And those decisions were not good for the club.

I hadn't thought about a couple of things. It's too bad, but this was really my first experience in taking the lead in an organization. Before this, I had always been able to decide to do something and then do it. When there was work that I felt needed to be done, I just went ahead and did my work. I found out that Dave had not learned about working in that kind of way. The first problem that I noticed was that Dave's lack of aggressiveness also meant that he was uncomfortable with the club growing very fast and with letting me be in charge of building it. He was not the kind of person who could let other people suggest something good and then just get out of the way and let them do it. His buddies were the Nomads, a group of aging Mongols who didn't actively participate in the club anymore—they didn't have to pay dues, didn't have to respond to calls or anything. They mostly just sat on the couch like Mr. Rogers and bitched about everything that was happening with the club.

What Dave didn't realize was that he couldn't stop the club from growing. There were just too many good people, strong people, who wanted to be Mongols. Just as important, other people were noticing that all of a sudden there were a lot more Mongols riding around—not just other motorcycle clubs, but they were the first ones we had to deal with. They began to challenge us, and you can't back down from that kind of challenge, or you'll wind up with twenty-five couch potatoes again. Being a Mongol means you always stand your ground and you are always ready to defend yourself when threatened. It also meant, now, that if you wanted to do something, you didn't stop to ask if anybody objected.

I knew things were going to go bad when we had the problem with the Arizona chapter. Arizona is a big stronghold for the Hells Angels, but while Junior was in charge, he had started up a chapter there. And it was rough. There had always been problems with the Angels harassing our people. There would be little skirmishes from time to time, but our guys there never gave up. Then the Angels started to get to Dave. They kept telling him that if he kept up the Arizona chapter, there was going to be a problem, and I think Dave took that personally, like they were going to go after him.

Maybe he didn't realize that he had the whole club, which was now full of very fearless people, to back him up. In the years before I joined the club, most of the really hard-core warriors, the ones who had faced down the Angels, had left the Mongols because the club was so fucked up. Dave didn't really know the new members. He didn't try to mingle with them, so he probably didn't realize that he had this little army behind him. One of the things I learned on the street is that you don't need a hundred, two hundred people to defend yourself. All you need is ten really top guys, ten guys who won't stand down no matter what happens to them. It's really amazing what you can do with just a few as long as they are people who will never, ever quit.

Anyway, Dave decided to close down the Arizona chapter. And

there was an uproar. The members in California didn't want to shut it down, and the members in Arizona didn't want to shut it down. But Dave just didn't have it, so he shut it down. Not only was this move unnecessary and wasteful, it made the Mongols look bad. From then on, I knew that Dave would have to go. Until then, I would keep with my program. But I knew that if I was going to succeed, the club would need to have strong leaders as well as strong members.

ne of the things I wanted to do was to increase the number of club members in Northern California. We were up to twenty chapters in Southern California, but I knew that it would make a big difference if we could expand up north.

I also knew that the Hells Angels considered Northern California their territory. They were very strong in Oakland and San Francisco—Oakland was Sonny Barger's, the Angels' president, chapter for most of the time he was in the Angels. So I started to take some trips up to that area. I had people who had cousins up there, and they gave me their addresses and I went up there and visited. I would rent a van—with my own money, not the club's—and some of the Pico chapter members would go up there with me. We would visit with the cousins and get to know them and maybe sleep in their garages. But if it was a family and we didn't want to intrude on them, we might spend the night outside in the van, turning it on every once in a while so that the heat would come on. We had some cold nights in those vans.

During the day I would also visit motorcycle shops and shows, just like I did when I learned about the Mongols. I started putting out feelers and asking other people who were going up north to look for the kind of biker who would be a Mongol. It was going to take somebody with balls to go ahead and fly the Mongol colors where there were a lot of Hells Angels. I needed to make sure that the people in the new chapter would be not only willing but able to take anything the Angels were going to give out. And then give it back to them twice as hard.

I started finding out about different groups—that is, a group of guys who rode together, not a formal club—and which ones had problems with the Hells Angels. When I was asking about these things, a lot of people would get leery and back off. They didn't want to talk to me because they knew that even though we weren't at war just then, the Hells Angels and the Mongols weren't the best of friends.

Oddly enough, I met the people I needed in Tijuana. Every year, we join in with other clubs and take toys to the children in Tijuana. So this one year, I ran into a group of about ten to fifteen guys who had come down from San Jose. I liked them, and when I checked, there were people to vouch for them. A few of the San Jose bikers in that group were white, but most of them were Hispanic. The Hells Angels still weren't actively recruiting Hispanics into the club because of the *Queen Mary* incident. The Hells Angel who had been killed at the *Queen Mary* show was Hispanic, one of the few in their club at the time.

So then I really wanted to show these guys what a great club the Mongols were. We starting renting a bigger van, one that could hold fifteen people, and I would take the whole Pico chapter up there. We'd hang out together, drink some beer, get to know one another, and of course talk about the club—how it was run, what it meant to be a Mongol, everything.

At some point I asked them if they were willing to start a Mongols chapter in San Jose. They said, "Hell, yes." The Hells

Angels had a chapter in San Jose, and they did not want us up there at all. It was their worst nightmare, because they basically controlled that area. So I gave the new guys a little speech. "There is a good chance that you are all going to have to defend yourselves just for existing up here," I said. "If you become a Mongol chapter, you will have to defend your brothers and stand up for the club no matter who attacks you. You have to keep the chapter going." They understood and they were ready; all of them said they wanted it.

I couldn't tolerate a chapter shutting down just because somebody attacked it. The only way we could continue to gain strength was to continue to be strong. It's that kind of world. Our reputation is what brings us members, and our reputation is that we won't quit until we're dead. After Dave shut down the Arizona chapter, I vowed to myself that I would never let a national pres shut down a chapter I had started.

I'm not sure if I can make it clear to people who don't live in this world or didn't grow up in my world just how dangerous our move north was. Once the Hells Angels discovered that we were starting a new chapter on their turf, they would consider it an attack, and they would definitely fight back. Someone would be stabbed; someone would be shot. That is the way our world is. If other clubs sense weakness in the Mongols, they will attack. If we started a chapter in San Jose and the Hells Angels killed everybody in it—and they are capable of that—then I would find five more guys who would volunteer to move to San Jose and stay there. And five more and five more until the chapter was established.

But it's not only other clubs. If the police believe that they can persuade you or scare you or hurt you enough to talk about other members, they will do everything in their power to make that happen. Police harassment is part of the life of every Mongol, as I've said. So I'm very straight when I talk to people about coming in. They must know and they must be ready for it. You have to tell them everything or it won't work.

Once the San Jose group committed, I went to Long-haired Dave, saying that we had the people to start a chapter in San Jose. Dave hemmed and hawed. "Look," he told me, "they're up there and we're down here and we don't violate each other's space." That was bullshit. I knew he was thinking about Arizona. I would remind him that the Angels had chapters in San Diego, San Bernardino, Orange County, and the San Fernando Valley. "They're already down here," I told him. "Why shouldn't we be able to start a chapter up there?" He would make some lame excuse about how those chapters opened a long time ago, or they were started when the Mongols weren't strong enough to fight them, and so on and so on. I didn't really see what difference that made. The bottom line was that the chapters existed, so there was no reason that we couldn't have chapters existing up north. I tried to remain respectful to my national pres, but I reminded him that our bottom rocker says "California," not "Southern California."

It's my opinion that Dave was just scared. He knew that the Hells Angels were going to be pissed off, so there would probably be trouble like there had been in the past—shootings, stabbings, dynamite. It wasn't so much because he was worried about being voted out of office, it was because he knew he would be a target. Let's face it, they usually go after the head guy. Dave wasn't the only one who didn't want the San Jose chapter to start. A lot of the Nomads were afraid. They had been through the war and knew what was coming down.

It was a frustrating time for me, and it went on forever. I kept telling Dave that the San Jose guys were ready, and then I would have to explain to them why things were taking so long. The guys up in San Jose weren't scared and they weren't impatient. They were cool about it and they understood that it would happen sooner or later. I gave them my word on it.

The older guys were also dragging their feet about new chapters and new members down south because they knew I was becoming more powerful with every person I brought in. Each new member was one more person who would support me. The old-timers would rather be big fish in a small pond, even when they could have been big fish in a big pond.

But the pond was getting bigger no matter what they did. People were really starting to notice that the club was becoming different, that we were having great parties. That was not only bringing new people in, but even bringing back some of the old members. One guy, Roger Pinney, hadn't come to any of the club events in years, but he started coming around again. It turned out that he had stopped coming because he thought the old leadership was so fucked up. He liked to party and we became friendly. I would talk to him and to JC about my frustrations with the club, but I still didn't want to go against any of the rules. What's the use of being a president of an organization if you don't respect your own rules?

It was now a year after I had first proposed the San Jose chapter to Dave, and he still avoided making a decision. I was getting really impatient. I told him straight out that he was not cutting it. Finally, at a meeting, I made a little speech about what was going on, and things became heated. Dave had gotten accustomed to being the head of the Mongols, so he stood his ground and got all the other old-timers worked up. They were all yelling about the five-year rule, and I said, OK, no problem, I understand. I remember looking at Dave and saying, "Do you want to let the members decide? Let them vote on who they want." Dave just turned his back on me, which was disrespectful. At least he could have answered.

But he was my national president, and I stayed with the program. I was not going to break a rule that the club had established, but I was not going to let Dave continue either. So I talked to JC and we went to Roger, who had been in the club for five years even before he stopped coming to meetings, and we asked him if he would run.

"I don't know how to run the club," he said. "I just like to come to the parties. I don't wanna run the club."

JC looked at me and nodded, so I said, "Don't worry about it. JC and I will help you run the club."

"Naw, look, I don't know a fucking thing about it."

"That doesn't matter, Roger," I said. "JC and I will do all the work. We just need somebody who will let this club grow."

"Well, isn't that kind of playing a trick on the guys? They oughta know who they're really voting for."

"No problem, Roger," I said. "We'll just tell 'em."

"OK," he said finally. "Let's do it." We shook hands on it. So JC nominated Roger, and Roger got up and said to everybody, "OK, look, I'm going to run for pres, but it's really going to be Doc and JC who are going to run the club. I mean, if you vote for me, you're really voting for Doc." Nobody objected.

It turned out that three people were nominated. Poor Boy, who had been in the club for maybe thirty years, was national vice president at the time and was basically a good guy. In fact, he proved it by having so little confidence in Dave that he decided to run against him. So it was Dave, Poor Boy, and Roger.

On the first election ballot, we just have a show of hands. Dave had some supporters from among the old guard, and Poor Boy had some too. But there was no question that Roger had won; so many hands went up that there were even a few little cheers. But because Dave and his crew were still officially in control, they were the ones counting the votes. So suddenly they said, "Oh wait, we messed up the counting. It doesn't add up to the right number. We'll have to do it again." Now this was obviously unfair; our side obviously had more votes, period. To say that we really had 115 instead of 120 wouldn't make any difference.

But we were still playing by their rules—even if they were changing them as they went. They got into a little huddle, Dave and Poor Boy and the other older guys, and when they broke up, suddenly Poor Boy was no longer a candidate. He must have agreed to drop out so that the older guys' votes wouldn't be split between him and Dave. That was the sort of shit they used to pull all the time, but I just let it go for the good of the club. I try not to bring it up unless it's tossed at me first. I could easily have had some guys thrown out of the club at that point. I wouldn't do that, but I never forgot who did what.

We won anyway, and by a pretty large margin. That was the beginning of the end of Long-haired Dave in the club. He didn't wind up in jail or anything, and he didn't resign from the club. He just kind of slunk away and hung with the Nomads. He still showed up at meetings now and then, but he rarely had anything to say, even if anybody had been interested in what it might be.

So we were in charge now, JC and me in reality, but Roger was the one who held the title. I thought that was best anyway, because Roger mainly just liked to drink, and people were always buying drinks for the national pres. I immediately assumed all the responsibilities of running the club—people came to me with questions—and JC became the national vice president. They asked me what I wanted to be, and I said I didn't need a title. I didn't care—I just wanted to create this monster club—but they insisted. They finally came up with national sergeant at arms, since I didn't want

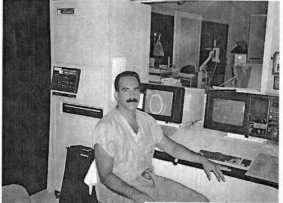

I spend my nights working as a radiologic technologist at Los Angeles County USC Medical Center. Everyone there knows about my work with the Mongols—some of them have come to Mongol parties.

My son—Ruben Jr., better known as Little Rubes—has been with me his whole life. This picture was taken when he graduated from kindergarten, when I was about twenty-three. I have no pictures from my own childhood because cameras were very rare in the neighborhoods where I grew up.

I have lived with my brother, Al, known as Al the Suit, most of my life.

Little Rubes was about four when I acquired this jack-in-the-box from a Jack in the Box restaurant. I had just been released from jail, and even though I didn't have any money, I wanted to bring him a present.

JC *(left)* has always been one of my most trusted advisers. Here he is with Little Rubes.

Cuete *(second from right)* is one of the smartest and toughest men I know. He is both my top adviser and my strongest soldier. He is standing here with Little Rubes, Shorty (who is doing time for allegedly killing the two Hells Angels in Laughlin, Nevada), and Al the Suit.

One of the best things about being a Mongol is riding your bike out on the open road. This picture was taken about a dozen years ago.

This is a more recent photo, with my current bike, a custom-built chopper.

This is the house I was living in when the police raided me in 2004. I was sleeping in my bedroom, on the right side of the second floor, when a police grenade exploded in my backyard. The double rows of concrete and steel-reinforced pillars were added later, to help prevent vehicles carrying explosives from entering.

Being hassled by the police is part of my life.
They stop me with guns in their hands, even when I am completely unarmed.

In the summer of 2007, my brother, Al, was driving on the freeway when a car pulled up next to him, lowered a window, and opened fire with an automatic weapon. Al was hit in the arm and the bullet lodged in his chest, but he was still able to pull off the freeway and make it to a gas station.

When one of us is in a situation where his life might be in danger, we organize what we call a response team. This is a team we organized for a meeting during our negotiations with the Mexican mafia. *Standing:* Gordy, Mac, Chickies, me, Little Rubes, Al, and Big Dog. *Kneeling:* Largo and Monstro.

Before the incident at the casino in Laughlin, I was trying to bring all the clubs together to increase cooperation and communication. A bunch of us had a great time with the Outlaws at their clubhouse in Oklahoma.

Bronson both looked and acted like the actor Charles Bronson, but he was a brave man who loved being a Mongol.

When we bury one of our members, it can be an impressive sight. After the memorial words, we all help in the burial itself, covering our brother with earth.

The shoot-out at the Flamingo Hotel and Casino in Laughlin, Nevada, was one of our toughest moments. Three people, one Mongol and two Hells Angels, were killed. The Mongol was Bronson *(top)*. The Hells Angels were Robert Emmet Tumelty *(middle)* and Jeramie Dean Bell *(bottom),* who was carried out to the driveway by EMT personnel and left there when he died. These are still images taken from the surveillance cameras operating in and around the casino.

Patches of the other most influential motorcycle clubs in the world *(clockwise from upper left):* the Bandidos, the Hells Angels, the Outlaws, the Pagan's, and the Sons of Silence. As you can see, the clubs have become international.

to be in charge of the money. But we assigned two members, Little Dave and Turtle, to perform the duties of national sergeant.

So at last, after almost two years, I was able to go up north and give patches to the San Jose chapter. At first they didn't fly the colors a lot, because we wanted to see how things were going to shake out. There was going to be violence, but we wanted to be in control of where and how it happened. Things were going beautifully because the guy leading San Jose, Datas, was a brave man. They started up in San Jose with about twelve or fifteen members, and even in the first month, before they had really been out and about yet, the Hells Angels were already threatening. They contacted me and I agreed that we needed to talk.

We would fly into an airport, say San Jose or San Francisco. Airports and casinos were considered safe because of security people and cameras. They might only be flying from Oakland, but that meant that everybody would have to get through the security screening, and that meant that none of us were carrying weapons. The security wasn't great back then, but it was still difficult to get a weapon through. If you really wanted to whack somebody, it doesn't matter where you are, but neither we nor the Angels were really there to cause injury. So we would fly into the San Jose airport, get off the plane, and meet in one of those food places inside the airport to talk.

There wasn't really a lot of negotiation. They would say, "This isn't going to happen," and we would say, "Yes it is," and they would say, "Why don't you guys stay where you belong?" and we would say, "We are." We just went back and forth like that. Then they produced this fake list of what they said was agreed to after the first war—including that we wouldn't start a chapter in their area. I couldn't believe they would try to pull shit like that.

It went that way for a little while. There had been a couple of other meetings when one of our guys was attacked outside of Hollister, which is way out in the middle of nowhere about ninety miles southeast of San Francisco. He was about sixty years old, from the north, and they caught him at a gas station and beat the crap out of him. This was the first act of violence between us. They didn't put him in the hospital, but they hurt him pretty bad. At the next meeting between me and the Hells Angels, they gave me some of his stuff, a ring of his and something from his vest. I went ballistic when I saw his stuff in their hands. I guess he'd lost it in the scuffle, but all I could think was, *Once you put your hands on a Mongol, there is going to be a problem.*

There was going to be a problem because I knew they weren't going to leave it alone and we were going to defend ourselves. So I started to plan. My thinking was that we had the chapter in San Jose, and that was what we wanted. So our best plan was simply to stand our ground. They were going to try to make us leave, but I would hold off fighting them outright as long as I could. To keep the chapter and not create waves was my goal. It's like robbing a bank—you don't want to call attention to yourself once you've got the money.

The way it usually works with those clubs is you try and talk it out. If you don't reach an agreement, the next step usually is you cut off communications, and once you cut off communications you know there's going to be a problem. They cut it off.

On the street, things were getting tenser. The chapter had a couple of run-ins with Angels, and there were a couple of fights. They beat up one of our members and one of their members got stabbed. But it had not gotten serious yet. That is, no one had been killed. One of our guys found some dynamite under his van, but he disposed of it without getting hurt.

One of the biggest motorcycle events in San Jose, maybe even

Northern California, is called the Blessing of the Bikes. A priest actually blesses the bikes. I don't know who started it, but it had always been a very big Angels event. You'd be surprised how many of these blessings happen all around the country every year. The one in San Jose happens during Easter, and it's become a little festival. The San Jose chapter told me that they wanted to go, flying the colors. Because San Jose was the first chapter to go into what used to be exclusive Angels territory, I really wanted to protect it at all costs until it was really going, and because it was still so new I didn't want to risk losing it. Even though those guys were brave, I felt that if somebody was going to get stomped, I should be the one. I said to them, "Look, I'm going to go in there first. I'll take one other person with me, and we'll see what happens. If we get stomped, at least the chapter doesn't take the beating and can come back another day. If it looks OK, you guys can go out in force."

At the Blessing of the Bikes, they close off the streets in one part of town, maybe four square blocks, and only allow bikes, no cars. The cops are sitting around in patrol cars, but since the Hells Angels had ruled this event, there hadn't been any major battles. Other clubs come in too, as long as they don't challenge the Angels, and they barbeque and party. The Angels aren't threatened by these small clubs. They are threatened by Mongols. Vendors come and set up stands to sell motorcycle paraphernalia. It's like a street fair, but for bikers.

The plan was that another brother and I would get to the edge of the fair and put on our Mongol patches, walk down the street to the center of the action, and see what happened. We'd carry walkie-talkies and have some backup, so if things started to look really dangerous and we were still able to talk, we could radio for a car to come in and pick us up. If it could reach us. When you have a couple hundred Hells Angels in a few square blocks, you never know what might go down if they get crazy. I had the San Jose chapter waiting in a house nearby. They were eager to show, but I had ordered them to stand down.

I met up with the other Mongols early. It's probably a good thing that I didn't know they had been partying all night and hadn't had any sleep. They looked like they always look. I saw Monster, and he's about my size and completely crazy, so I decided I'd see if he wanted to walk into a den of Hells Angels with me. "Hey, bro," I said, "you bring your patch?"

"Yeah, I did."

"Want to wear it?"

"Hell, yes." He smiled. "What's the plan?"

"The plan is that you and I are going to walk down to the party."

"Fuck. You're my pres. I got your back."

I thought that was pretty cool. He didn't have to think about it. "All right, bro, it's on."

While another bro drove us down to the event, I told Monster the rest of the plan and explained that Mike and some other guys would be standing by as backup, not wearing their colors. When we got out of the car, we were on a side street where the vendors were and some barbecues. One club had one of those fifty-gallon drums cut in half as a barbecue, and they had a ton of meat cooking on it. And there were Hells Angels all over—you could tell by their red and white colors. As we walked down the street, everything stopped and it got totally quiet. With each step we took, the quiet went a step farther with us. People just stopped and stared. They were really amazed to see Mongols there.

So we walked into the middle of the main intersection and stopped to see what would happen next. Hells Angels began to walk to one corner. There was a park behind us where kids were playing and people were barbecuing. Their motorcycles were lined up right there. The Hells Angels began to form a line across the intersection, and pretty soon I saw nothing but a wall of red and white.

I turned around to see if we were being surrounded, and the street behind us was completely deserted. Where there had been seventy-five or a hundred people, there was no one. Even that fifty-gallon-drum barbecue was completely gone, like it had never been there. The only sounds came from the police squad cars backing the hell out of there as fast as they could go. The police will not get in the way of two biker clubs fighting. They will get in the middle of a lot of stuff, but not two biker clubs. They're afraid.

"I wish I'd brought a knife," I said to Monster.

"A knife, hell. A grenade."

The Hells Angels hadn't known we were going to do this, but it almost looked like they expected us. The Angels standing around us were huge. Monster and I are both six-foot-two, and Monster thinks they were four, five inches taller than we are and built like wrestlers. I was thinking that if I took a hard-enough beating, I could die there. Being booted in the head when you're a youngster is one thing, but at my age it could kill me. I could see their guns in their waistbands. I checked in with the backup team. They'd been busted by the police. "Monster," I said, "it's just you and me now."

"Way it goes, Doc."

Someone in the crowd on the opposite corner yelled, "You're not welcome here."

Monster and I just stared at them. We had what I call our war faces on. Then I said, "We're not going anywhere." They were still building up, but I'll tell you, you reach a point when you're a Mongol, you kind of believe you can take anything. You honestly believe that no matter what anyone does to you, you will somehow come out on top.

"Hey, Doc," Monster says.

"What?"

"You know, we're gonna get the beating of our lives here."

"We'll see."

"So what I'd really like to do right now is to give them the finger."

"Don't. Neither of us has a weapon."

"Doc, I'd rather get my ass kicked by the Angels than by the Mongols."

"What?"

"When the brothers find out I didn't mess with these fuckers, they're gonna stomp me."

"Just stand still. Do what I do."

There was nothing behind us and a wall of Hells Angels in front of us. It was so quiet you could hear the camera shutters clicking away. There were professional photographers on the roof, I could see them. People were taking pictures of the two Mongols who were about to get beaten up. I don't know if they were working for law enforcement or the newspapers, but I could hear the shutters clicking. Now that we had been challenged, we had to stay, at least until we'd proved our point. Even though it was two against whatever, it didn't matter. So we're standing there and looking at all these Hells Angels and we're staring at them and they're staring at us.

But it wasn't like the Old West, where at some point we would have to draw our guns. All I wanted to do then and there was to prove that we weren't going to run from the Angels. If they wanted to challenge us, if they wanted to fight, that was fine. But I didn't need to start a fight. After a while, when it was clear that the Angels weren't actually going to do anything, I walked over to the curb. Next to them.

I stood there for a second or a minute—I'm not sure, I lost track of time—and then some of the Angels started walking toward us.

These were their ultimate fighters, I guess, with the leather and the spikes. And they walked up to us so close that we could feel it as they passed. But they walked right by without touching us. I guess they wanted to see if we would react, if we would panic and start something, but of course we were not going to show any weakness at all.

Monster says that about this time, he saw Sonny Barger escorted out of there. I didn't see that. We stood there until it was clear that we weren't going to run. And then I said, "Let's go," and we walked through them. As I walked away I didn't know if I was going to feel a set of brass knuckles or a ball-peen hammer on my head. We walked up the sidewalk for about a block and a half, when one of our cars, which had gotten away from the police, came by and picked us up.

Twenty minutes later we returned with the chapter on bikes.

8

Two Steps Forward, One Step Back

mage is everything. We had given everyone in San Jose the idea that we were not afraid of the Angels. The reputation of the Mongols grew, because people knew that we would stand behind our members in any fight with the Angels. The San Jose chapter added new members and started to ride everywhere, but the Hells Angels didn't try any open confrontation. I knew that this was not the end of it, but I also knew that there would always be fights between us and the Angels—at least until they gave up the idea that they had the right to tell other people what to do.

I was also able to right another wrong by giving the Arizona chapter a new life. From my point of view, everything was going very well. Roger was staying out of our way, doing what he does best—drinking. I kept on thinking of new ways we could expand the club. I was beginning to see that our growth was creating some new problems. We were in a tense situation with the Angels, and the cops were hassling us all the time. I had been able to cut down on the amount of fighting and stuff like that, but the more Mongols there were, the more Mongols there were for the cops to hassle. Also, I could see the cops had the idea that we were gangbangers, and they figured we had to be doing something illegal. They knew me and they knew a lot of the guys in the club from the days when we were gangbanging, and they just assumed that we were still doing the same things, but calling ourselves Mongols instead of Avenues or what have you.

Now, I'm not saying that there weren't people in the club who were still carrying on, and there was no way that I could ride herd on each and every one of these guys. It's not something I wanted to do, and let's face it, it's not something I could do. I would just be driving them out of the club—or they would be driving me out of the club. But we made it a rule that if you were breaking any laws, you had better not be wearing your colors doing it. We had to discipline Monster because there was a shootout in his living room one time. He brought somebody to his house who was not a Mongol, but who was carrying a weapon. We took away his officer bars for that—we have a rule that no guns are allowed at any Mongol meeting or party. We'll take the gun away and return it to the individual—empty—afterward.

Anyway, the police were noticing us, and the Hells Angels were sure noticing us, and it seemed to me that we should build up our communication with other clubs. As I said, if you're not in contact with people, that often leads to problems. I wanted to see if we could work out a deal so that, as the Mongols started chapters in new places, we wouldn't be going to war with every other motorcycle club. I wanted to get hold of the heads of all the other clubs and create a relationship. I thought that if I could just explain who we were, I could make them understand that even though we were growing, we were not going out there to annihilate them. I wanted us to be able to visit their areas without creating trouble, and for them to be able to come into ours.

I called Frank Vital, the head of the Outlaws, which began in Illinois, and George Wegers, the head of the Bandidos, which is based in Texas primarily. Some of them are pretty well off and have these huge ranches, with lions and tigers. I said maybe we could have a few beers together sometime, like that. I actually was invited to the Outlaw clubhouse in Oklahoma. They invited us to a party there, treated us good, and then there was a moment when we all sat down together and one of the Outlaws just said very bluntly, "What is it you guys want?" See, for us to come out of nowhere and just show up and be friendly was so rare that they didn't know what to make of us. I told him that we just wanted to get to know them. We were known as an East L.A. club, but now we were branching out, but not in an antagonistic way. And it all went very well.

We actually had a chapter in Oklahoma, so I visited them while I was there. It was very small, but it was alive. The only other Mongol who had ever visited was Junior—and he'd demanded that they pay his way. So I visited them and I encouraged the California brothers to go there too. There started to be a real exchange between us, which was really important because these guys were out there doing what had to be done as Mongols but no one ever acknowledged them. I think they have gone from five or six members to almost fifty members now.

Pretty soon we had Outlaws and Bandidos and Pagans all coming to our parties from time to time, and once we got to know one another we weren't so distrustful. We had a decent relationship with everybody except the Hells Angels, who would send messages telling us things like if we let the Outlaws come to Los Angeles, there was going to be a big problem. I guess they were afraid that we were trying to build some kind of alliance against them, which is what law enforcement was saying too. Maybe they thought we really were Mongols and I was Genghis Khan trying to take over the world.

But that's ridiculous, of course. First, you couldn't get everybody to do that; it's completely against the spirit of the clubs. Each one is very independent minded and every member is very loyal to his club. Second, when you are a major club you don't accept help from anybody else. Remember what happened to Satan's Slaves when they asked the Hells Angels for help against the Mongols? Our feeling is, if you can't handle it yourself then step out of the way. The Mongols never for a second thought they needed help against the Hells Angels. It's actually an insult to think that we would go to anybody else for help.

All we were doing was reaching out to these guys, and we found a lot in common with a lot of them. A majority of club members everywhere just want to ride their motorcycles and have a good time. As long as you respect one another, you can survive side by side, for the most part. If, for instance, the Bandidos wanted to start a chapter in California, there would be a discussion about that—but there would be a discussion, not a war.

During this time, JC and I were beginning to realize that Roger was becoming a problem. He still liked to drink as much as ever, but somehow he began to think that he should be making decisions. Once again, we gave someone power and that person decided he knew better than the members. Unfortunately, his decisions were usually not very good for the club. He started doing things that were a real problem for the club. For one, he liked to start fights. He had a lot of balls, but because he didn't grow up on the streets, he was not very smart about when to fight. He would mix it up with whoever was around—not with Mongols, with civilians. And if a president gets in a fight, everyone around has to back him up.

Roger gathered a group of brothers around him and started hanging out at bars, getting drunk, and trying to start trouble. As long as he had enough of his people behind him to make him feel tougher than he was, he acted tough. Whenever a fight did break out, he always let his cronies take the brunt of it while he walked away without a scratch. That didn't sit very well with the other Mongols.

One time on a run to Tijuana we were in a club that had a second-floor balcony overlooking the street. As it happened, there were a couple of East L.A. baldies—gangsters—drinking below us. Roger thought it would be funny to flick ice chips off the balcony onto their bald heads.

"What the fuck are you doing?" I said to him as I took his glass of ice chips away.

"Who gives a fuck, Doc?" he said. "There's two hundred of us and only six of them."

That was just the kind of thing that could touch off exactly what we didn't need—a major new battle zone right in our own backyard. Our hands were full enough with Hells Angels from the north; we didn't need a local turf war with the gangs over something as stupid as this.

In a way, the worst thing of all was that, one night, one of Roger's girlfriends, a stripper, got drunk and slapped him across the face in public. We didn't like the idea of people saying that the national president of the Mongols had been slapped by his woman. A couple of weeks later, she was arrested and tried to make a deal with the law where she would name Mongol names and match them with whatever kind of crime they wanted to charge us with, as long as she could then be put in the witness protection program. She must have been desperate to get away from Roger. Luckily—for her, far more than for us—nothing came of it.

Around that time, I was talking with a biker named Silver (Roy

Hill) who wanted to start a new chapter in Carson City, Nevada. He had a good friend who was a Mongol, and that person vouched for him, but I knew it wasn't going to be easy. The Hells Angels had visited him at his home and said they'd kill him if he even tried it. I told him to go ahead and put together the chapter and that Roger and I would come to Carson City and make him and his friends Mongols.

Silver found some guys who were willing, and Roger, JC, and I went out there to see them. We stayed overnight in a hotel, and the next morning JC and Roger and I met downstairs. JC said to me, "It ain't gonna happen, Doc."

I couldn't believe what I was hearing. "What do you mean, it ain't gonna happen?"

"It's too dangerous," Roger said. "What happens if we have to shut it down, like we had to do with Arizona?"

I said, "No, no, no." I was feeling desperate. "Wait a minute, you're crazy. These guys are committed. We can do it." We went and sat down, and as the three of us were talking, Silver came walking by. I called him over and asked him to tell Roger and JC how he felt.

"I want to be a Mongol," he said without hesitating. They looked at him and looked away, like they didn't know what to say, and Silver said, "If you don't let me be a Mongol here, I'll move to California to be a Mongol."

"You hear the dedication," I practically shouted. "Do you hear this man? He wants to be a Mongol." There I was, arguing with my own club to let this happen. I had already decided that if we started the chapter and Silver got weak, I would come back myself with a couple of others. We would just move there and stay until it took off again. I was committed and determined and I would not allow it to shut down.

Finally they agreed to let him start the chapter. It was hard. I remember when we officially opened the chapter I went up with some other Mongols to celebrate at a local bar and some Hells Angels showed up to try to kick us out. A brawl broke out and one of their guys' rockers got ripped off and disappeared.

The next day someone called me without identifying himself and said the Hells Angels wanted their rocker back. I told them we didn't have it. They didn't believe me, but as it turned out, one of the law enforcement officers who'd been called to break things up had found it and taken it home with him as a souvenir. His supervisors eventually made him give it back, a rare demonstration of honesty on their part, which prevented a lot of trouble going down between the Mongols and the Nevada Highway Patrol. Most of the time they take "souvenirs," things that belong to us, rings, lighters, pictures, statues, all kind of paraphernalia, without reporting it. This time we got lucky and he didn't keep it.

Silver really went through hell. The Angels would drive by his house and fire off a few shots. One time they came onto his property with a gun, and he had to wrestle it away from them. He would call me every day and tell me what had happened that day. "They're the masters of intimidation," I told him, "but they won't keep it up. Keep a grip on your gun and just relax, because it's going to work out. I saw it happen up north. Sit tight."

Three months later, six of Silver's Nevada Mongols were jumped by fourteen Hells Angels in downtown Reno, and the Angels got their asses kicked but good. The Mongols were in Nevada to stay. A week later, the Hells Angels clubhouse there was shot up.

The last straw with Roger was when we went to Colorado. We'd had a few members in Colorado for about ten years, but they weren't flying their colors because nobody official had visited there—which shows you what kind of leadership we had. They needed the support, because a club called the Sons of Silence was there in force, and that is a respected club. I got hold of Terry, the national president of the Sons. I told him that we were going to come out in the open there, and Terry listened and responded very evenly and intelligently. He would say things like, "I'm not sure if that's the best idea," but we continued to talk. We had four or five conversations on the phone, and finally he said, "Well look, Doc, I will take this to my club, but before I do that I want to meet with you in person. Meeting a person says a lot," he went on. "One, that you have the balls to step over here, and two, that you stand behind your word."

That was fine with me; I feel the same way. I knew that I would have to take Roger along, but I would figure out a way to handle that. We agreed to meet at a Harley run that was going to be held in Four Corners, where Colorado, Arizona, New Mexico, and Utah meet.

So I went there with Roger, JC, and Mike Munz. We were going to meet Terry at a large resort—lots of rooms and a central building that had a restaurant and a bar. We weren't really worried about having any trouble, but it's always smarter to meet in a very public place. We were staying in a little hotel a few miles away, so we rented a car and drove over to the resort.

It was infested with Hells Angels. As we drove up we could spot their prospects, whom they had posted as lookouts. They set off the alarm bells even before we had parked. As we drove through the complex we could see Hells Angels standing in their hotel rooms holding shotguns and rifles. The prospects were running through the resort, keeping up with us to see where we were going and what we were up to. There had to be a couple of hundred Angels there.

We said, "Fuck it, let's park." If we had to take them on, we would. We went inside and the first thing we saw was George Wegers, the head of the Bandidos. So we had a couple of beers with him and talked. Then Terry showed up and he turned out to be the nicest guy you could imagine. We sat and talked over everything. He continued to explain why he didn't think it would be a good idea for us to fly our colors in Denver, but he listened to us. We understood that he didn't want any problems with his members, or to alert law enforcement.

Finally he said, "How about this? You seem like decent people, so I don't have a big problem with you being here, but you have to fly Denver, not Colorado." That we just couldn't have. We had fought a war with the Angels in California over this, and it was just unacceptable for a major club like the Mongols to take a backseat to anyone. I would lose the respect of my membership if I allowed that to happen.

I said it at that meeting and I still say it to this day: I will never box my club into an agreement that cannot be honored. When I'm making an agreement I always think not only about the present day, but also ten years from now, twenty years from now. Thinking about what I wanted for the Mongols, I imagined a day when we had grown so big that we just couldn't accept the fact that we were second-class citizens in Colorado. Maybe the reason we were in a war with the Angels was that a long time ago, somebody made an agreement that was a burden to future generations. If I feel I'm putting Mongols in a situation that will be a problem in the future, I figure it's better to deal with the problem right away rather than let it fester. We were at war today because the Mongol Nomads had made bad agreements yesterday.

Unfortunately, Roger didn't understand that point of view. He said to Terry, "Okay, fine, I'll accept that." And he looked at me and kind of smiled and nodded as if he wanted me to go along with him. I thought to myself, *Oh god, you moron*. He wasn't even drunk then, he just didn't have the brains to think of anything but the present.

Luckily, all the rest of us were all on the same page. Mike Munz got right up, grabbed Roger by the arm, and said, "Come on, I want to talk to you." Then he yanked Roger out of his chair and dragged him away from the table. Mike's a big guy. If he really wants you to come with him, you have a hard time saying no. If you asked me whether a national pres should be treated this way, I would say that it's necessary when he's doing something that is not good for the club.

I turned back to Terry, who was a little surprised, and said, "Listen buddy, we've been through war with the Hells Angels. We have not backed down from anybody. We've paid our dues in this world. Are we not a major club?"

"Doc, I know about you guys. You're the real deal."

"Well, you wouldn't ask any other major club to do that. Knowing what you know about us, how could you ask us to settle for a city rocker?"

Terry stopped and he looked at me and he said, "You know what, Doc? You're right. Let me take it back to the membership." I said fine and we shook hands.

I don't know what Mike Munz told Roger. We never discussed it, but I think I have a good idea. Mainly, I was totally disgusted with Roger. He was making decisions that were really fucked up. When we got back to California, I sat down with him and I started to have discussions with him about it. I told him that I didn't care that he had the title, the deal was that JC and I would run the club. He complained that he was national president, not me, and I told him I didn't care. If he was going to screw things up, I wanted him to stay away from making decisions. "Just concentrate on the freebies, Roger," I said. "Let people buy you drinks and things, let the girls come on to you and make the most of it. But if you keep on screwing things up, I will have to do something about it."

"Are you threatening me, Doc?"

"I am reminding you that the members knew they were voting for me and JC when they cast their votes for you. If I tell them that you have become a problem, they will not be happy about that. They will take care of their business."

Roger quieted down, but it was obvious he wasn't happy. I didn't really care. I had learned something, though. The best leader is the one who comes into the job already having the respect and admiration of his people. He's somebody who doesn't get seduced by girls throwing themselves at him or people giving him free things and telling him that he's always right.

I got a call about a week later from Terry. "Doc, it's on. You guys are Colorado official." *Good for him,* I thought. *He's a smart man and a leader who deserves the respect he has.*

We went up there for the official patching-in ceremony, and an interesting thing happened. We went to dinner the day before the meeting, and while we were sitting down, Sonny Barger walked in with his huge entourage. As he walked by my table, he nodded his head to me. We took the risk and it was worth it. At that first encounter in San Jose, they had outnumbered us a hundred to one, but if you run out on things that are worth doing, you can't have any respect for yourself. And your club is never going to be about anything.

The year that had started out so well had turned into another difficult one. We had made a lot of progress, but I still felt like I was fighting my way through sand. Every time, it was two steps forward, one step back. Then we took a huge leap back with the Morongo Casino incident.

ne of our members, Rick Slaton, was a contestant in the Ultimate Fighting Championship, which is one of those matches where the contestants can pretty much do whatever they want to each other. There are a few illegal moves, but not very many, and these are not planned shows, like wrestling matches. One big event in the series was held at the Morongo Casino, which is about twenty miles west of Palm Springs, and naturally a lot of Mongols wanted to watch Rick fight. This was a big deal. There were a lot of us there right down in the front row cheering Rick, and we were having a good time watching the fight. Then Slaton got called for kneeing his opponent in the groin. We didn't mind the referee's call, but some people in the seats above us got upset about what Rick had done and started throwing their drinks at the ring.

Of course you can't throw a drink without it getting all over, and it got all over the Mongols at ringside. That did not go down well. Without the proper leadership, it turned into an all-out brawl. Naturally the Mongols gave as good as they got, and the casino called in the police. There were about a hundred cops there, according to the newspapers, and some of them carried M16 rifles.

It was a mess that never would have happened if the leader of the club had taken charge. Even Rick was yelling from the ring at people to stop fighting. Several people were injured, and quite a few Mongols were arrested. It made the news all over. It was stupid. I don't condone fighting like that, and I try to get people to think about what they're doing and to get the chapter presidents to think about what can happen. But I'm not a police officer and I can't chase the members around and tell them what they can or can't do. I'm still trying to this day to try to get everybody to cooperate to stay in control of themselves; I keep saying, "Listen, you don't have to go there. Everything that happens represents the club. Think about that."

I learned some things from Morongo, and I vowed that things would get better. But in fact, things were just about to get a lot worse.

9

Laughlin

ne of the biggest events during the year in the bike world is the annual run to the casinos in Laughlin, Nevada. For some reason, it just became the place where all the clubs went in the spring. It was started by a Harley dealer in 1983, and four hundred riders came the first year. Then it just grew and grew. The newspapers say that anywhere from forty thousand to eighty thousand bikers may show up. I think Nevada has something to do with it. Not just the promoters and the casinos, but the whole Nevada culture. The gun laws are easier, the driving laws are easier, and you're out there more or less in the middle of nowhere right down at the southern tip of Nevada.

We basically just take over the town for one continuous round-the-clock party from Thursday evening until Sunday. The town is not much more than a strip with casinos on one side, the Colorado River to the east, and nothing to the west. Over the years, certain clubs have taken certain hotels—the club goes to the same hotel every year, so it's known as their hotel. The Mongols had always stayed at the Riverside Resort Hotel and Casino, which is at the north end of the strip. Right next door to it is the Flamingo (now called the Aquarius), which has always been the Angels' hotel. I knew that would be a problem.

By 2002, the whole world knew that there was friction between us and the Hells Angels. The whole world including law enforcement. A lot had happened between us just in the last year or so. There had been the Blessing of the Bikes in San Jose and the rise of the Mongols' San Jose chapter. The Angels were tense about how the Mongols were growing anyway, so there had been a lot of little skirmishes between Mongols and Angels. Whenever we traveled in numbers anywhere, including on our own home turf, the police always showed up in force, on their bikes behind us to harass us.

So with the casinos, the clubs, and the police all knowing about the problems, you can imagine that law enforcement in Nevada and beyond was on high alert in 2002 for the Laughlin run. Everybody knew there was the possibility of serious trouble. We had been warned in Los Angeles that there were going to be a lot of cops in Laughlin that weekend. That meant everybody—local police, state police, ATF, FBI, you name it, they would be there.

I had been wracking my brain to figure out how to get the situation to cool down. It was getting into that kind of gangbanging mentality, where one side does something, so the other side responds, and it just keeps going back and forth until someone dies and the police make everyone's life miserable forever. So I was working with the heads of many of the major clubs—Outlaws, Bandidos, Vagos, and some others—trying to get them all to a meeting together to see if we could work things out so there would be no more problems like the ones in the past. Even the Hells Angels were to be included in this meeting, though I hadn't been in touch with them yet. It would be something no one had ever done before, but I was just thinking that I could save us a lot of distraction and pain and money. By the time we were leaving for Laughlin, I was just at the point where I thought I would be able to make it happen.

After Morongo, the last thing I wanted was more news stories about the Mongols beating up people and causing riots. We had the chapter in San Jose, so we had the goods. The idea was to stay out of the Angels' reach until the chapter was established and the Angels cooled off. Roger had been nothing but trouble for months, so I planned the strategy for the weekend.

I decided, for the first time in our history, that instead of staying at the Riverside—right next door to hundreds of Hells Angels—we would go all the way to the opposite end of the strip. That was Harrah's. Not only is Harrah's at the opposite end of the strip, but it's in a large pit. You have to drive down below the level of the main street in order to get into the parking lot and the entrance to the hotel. So I figured there was no way we were going to cross paths with the Angels accidentally if we stayed in Harrah's.

Next, I thought about how we were going to get there. Most of the clubs that go to Laughlin take Interstate 15 most of the way. It's almost unavoidable that we would run into Hells Angels on the road, and since there are really only a couple of places on that highway where people can gas up and have something to eat, we were certain to run into the Angels there too. Remember that we were going to be moving between one and two hundred members on this run. It would be like trying to hide an elephant. It wasn't that we were afraid of them; we were just using our brains—a war with the Angels could only hurt us and hurt San Jose.

So we decided that we would take a back route—Route 62 east until we got to Nevada 95 north. It's an untraveled road, which is what we wanted, but a lot of it is gravel. You can't imagine, unless you ride yourself, how awful it is to ride a motorcycle through gravel. Unless you're at the front, it's like being in combat. It's hot and dry, and you're trying to avoid potholes with a motorcycle two feet away on either side of you. You're being smacked with gravel that's going sixty miles an hour in one direction while you're going sixty miles an hour in the other. I felt like one of those guys in the tanks in the Sahara during World War II.

When you're moving that many bikes down a highway, especially on a bad road, you have to be very disciplined. All along the main pack we have road captains. Every five or six bike lengths you have a captain, and there's a front, a middle, and a tail to the pack. The road captains keep the pack together, they keep everybody moving as one. They're all in communication with one another, using hand signals. They signal when to slow down, speed up, watch out, go to the left, or go to the right. It's stressful because you can't stop and start and you can't communicate exactly what you want except with a lot of hand signals and a lot of yelling that nobody can hear because they're on their bikes. You know there's danger but you can't just yell, "Watch out!" The other part of the captains' job is to put themselves in harm's way. They're out there riding point, so to speak, and if there's a mechanical problem or if a bike goes down, they're on the spot.

It worked perfectly, despite all the complaining about the conditions, which I could understand even if I knew that the route was necessary. We traveled all the way up there without getting into a confrontation with anybody else. We came into Laughlin on Thursday from the south, where there are no casinos and so no bikers, and we landed at the casino at the opposite end from the Hells Angels. A lot of the guys wanted to ride down the main street all the way to the Flamingo, but I told them that was not part of the program this weekend.

But of course the Hells Angels had already started looking for us and found out what hotel we were using. When we got to Harrah's, there were four or five Hells Angels wandering around. They were probably like scouts, but immediately there were some arguments, some verbal confrontations, which I broke up as quickly as I could. I took the Hells Angels to the bar and I said, "Let me buy you a beer. We don't need any problems here. Let's take it easy." We talked for a few minutes while everybody calmed down and I made my position very clear to them, that we were not looking for any fights, that we didn't want to cross paths with them. If there were any misunderstandings, we would defend our members, but we were down at Harrah's just so that wouldn't happen.

I was on my guard the next day, watching everything, everybody. There were police everywhere, in the parking lot, riding up and down the street, on horses, on bikes, in cars and jeeps. Little Rubes was there with me, helping with the security, but most of the members were there just to party and have a good time. We had a couple of guys watching the bikes, and they had radios, but there were a lot of bikes and a lot of guys all over the place.

Friday went OK. The hotel provides a complete package and everything is set up for the bikers. They had a bar and a DJ and a dance floor in the courtyard of the hotel, so we could just stay there and party among ourselves. All our women were there, the weather was beautiful, and we were just having a good time.

Saturday night we were all outside in the courtyard when Roger decided that he wanted to visit another casino. JC and I tried to tell him that it was not a good idea; once we started to have people wandering around, it would be impossible to keep control of them. I said as forcefully as I could that we had everything we needed right there. I even talked with the management and they agreed to keep the DJ playing and the bar open as long as we were spending money. Two hundred Mongols will spend a lot of money, so management was happy and we were happy. "Roger, let's just stay where we are. We worked out a deal, the hotel is catering to us and giving us anything we want. Why do we need to go anywhere else?"

Of course he was in his decision-making mode by then and he'd had a lot to drink, so he was full-blown thinking he was running the program. "No, no, Doc. We're Mongols, so we go wherever we want to go, whenever." I would never outright refuse to go in that situation, because I'm a Mongol, and if my members are going, I'm going. Besides, I know that somebody has to keep an eye on things. With Roger in this mood, anything could happen, and it would probably be bad.

We went next door to the Palms, as a club. Most of the members went inside to party, but I stayed outside with Victor, a member of the Bandidos, looking around, keeping watch. While we were out there, law enforcement approached me. By this time of night, there were even more police than during the day, and they were going up and down the strip all the time. These cops weren't friendly, but they weren't acting like we'd already committed a crime either. After all, probably half the town's budget comes from the bikers who come for this weekend, and the police don't want to stir up the situation any more than the casino owners do. So they said, more or less, "We're really concerned that you guys are going to go down to the Flamingo and kick in some doors. We don't want that to happen."

"Look, guy, we're not going anywhere," I said as reasonably as I could. "That's the furthest thing from my mind. We're not here to make any trouble. I'm going to keep everybody off the strip this weekend."

I guess they felt reassured, because they backed off a little bit, but in the meantime there was a problem inside the casino. Somebody, a civilian, got socked by a Mongol, or at least that's what they told me. I finally got everybody to go back to Harrah's, but I was feeling more and more frustrated. I knew this was a stupid mistake. If Roger had just stuck with the plan, it wouldn't have happened. We were having a good time among ourselves; all of a sudden, we went outside, and we had a confrontation. I determined to watch even more carefully than before.

Back at our hotel, the party continued. Just after midnight or so, some of the members start to burn out from the long ride up. Mongol parties can easily go on through the next day without stopping, but some guys are older, and some have their wives with them or what have you. For whatever reason, about half of the club went up to their rooms to take a nap. About that time, the hotel security approached Roger and said, "We're going to start searching your people, so they need to take their weapons up to their rooms and put them away."

The hotel knows that the longer the night goes on, the more chance there is for trouble. The problem is that we know it too, or at least I know it. I knew from my old gangbanging days that you should never leave yourself defenseless. Maybe nothing will happen, but maybe something will, and it can be deadly. There were civilians in the casino, and our women were still around and some of the younger members—including Little Rubes, who wouldn't leave me anyway. I didn't want any of them hurt.

But Roger didn't have that experience, and Roger had appointed himself decision maker for the night. Unfortunately, Roger's decision was to agree, as always. He told Curly, as we call Ken Dysart, to go around and tell everybody to take their weapons up to their rooms. A lot of people groaned and protested. "No," Roger said, "you have to put them away because these guys are going to do random searches. They can bust you if you're holding." The guys knew that they should follow a direct order from their president. A few of them, because they've lived the life I've lived, kept their weapons. They didn't want to start trouble, but they wanted to be able to end it.

Roger was lulled into a feeling of safety because of the gauntlet of law enforcement on the strip. Not even these cops, he thought, could all be so incompetent that they wouldn't see the Hells Angels coming down the strip to our place. He figured the police would do just what they'd done when we went next door—approach the Angels and try to halt any kind of advance. "I'm not concerned," Roger told people. "I don't have anything on me, but over there I was surrounded by cops telling me that they don't want us in that other hotel. I have to imagine they are doing the same thing the opposite way."

Besides, a casino is just about the most-watched place in the world. There are cameras everywhere. *Everywhere.* You can't make a move in a casino without being caught on three different cameras. The Angels would have to be crazy to start anything as long as we stayed in the casino.

So there we were, maybe thirty or forty of us, mostly unarmed and having a good time. That room in Harrah's is basically a ring of slot machines and craps tables surrounding Rosa's Cantina, which has a big bar inside with walls around it and a little stand-up bar at the front where you can get drinks to carry around. Across from the stand-up bar is a cashier's cage. I was sitting at the slot machines talking with a couple of girls when I looked over toward the entrance.

A Hells Angel walked through the door.

I stopped playing for a minute, and as I watched, a few more walked in. There had been Hells Angels in Harrah's that night, and they had made some comments to our guys. We had been able to keep a lid on it so far. But these guys looked different. They didn't go to the slot machines or the pool tables, for one thing. For another, I could see they had weapons in their hands, not even concealed in a pocket or a waistband. Several of them were just holding a gun in front of them, one hand on the stock and the other hand covering the gun, maybe with their bandanna wrapped around it. Another one came through the same way, gun in his hand. Another came in with a ball-peen hammer. It doesn't take a gangster or a genius to know that when somebody walks into a casino with a weapon, and he knows that there are all those cameras running, this guy is not there to bullshit around. They intended to use those weapons.

In a split second, I got on the phone and contacted everybody. If I press a certain key on my phone, I can send a call to the head of every chapter. "I need every single man down here immediately. Bring your weapons." I knew that people would jump out of bed and head to the elevators. It wouldn't take long, but it would take a few minutes.

I looked at the Angels more closely. They were milling around the bar, getting drinks and looking around glassy eyed, keyed up. It was pretty obvious that they were on meth or something like that. These were not people you could reason with. While I was standing there, Roger came up and said to me, "What do you think? I think we should try to squash this," meaning he thought he could defuse the situation. Normally I would want to try that too, but at that moment, I was hardly even thinking, just reacting with my gangster instincts: *If it doesn't work, we are outnumbered and we are outgunned and we are dead.*

Everything in me, everything in my life, told me that you could not just smooth this over. It was 2:00 A.M. and these guys had come here to rumble, and they weren't thinking about anything else. I said to Roger, "No, sit back, look at these guys. They're not here to talk. They're not attacking yet, so let's just wait a few more minutes until the rest of the troops get down here with some straps."

Having more Mongols around meant we had two possibilities: on the one hand, we'd be negotiating from strength, so we had a better chance of avoiding trouble. On the other, if these knuckle-heads didn't want to make peace, then we'd be able to whip the shit out of them. Honestly, it didn't matter to me which happened. Obviously, peace was better than war, but I can't lie to you and say that I wanted peace at any cost. If they didn't want peace, then I would rather stomp them.

"Let's go talk to them," Roger said.

"No. Roger, these guys are tweaking. They're looking for trouble. There's nothing to talk about."

"We need to do something before it's too late."

"It's too late already, Roger. Look, they're high, they've got their weapons in their hands, they want to start a fight. We need our people here and we need them together so we can face these guys down." He wasn't bright enough to read the writing on the wall. We had an argument, but it had to be quick because Hells Angels were streaming into the casino now. Roger basically said, "Fuck you," and walked away toward the Angels at the bar. Roger asked for Pumper and JT to go with him to watch his back. I stayed right with him, but as we approached the Hells Angels, two Mongols, one of them a sergeant at arms, started arguing with each other. One guy was yelling, "Get back, get out of the way," and the other one was saying, "Fuck you," and a fight was about to erupt between them.

I stopped right there. I didn't want them fighting each other, but that wasn't the only reason I stopped. I knew that what Roger was doing just wasn't very smart. I was pretty sure that someone was going to get shot or stabbed, and I was the one who needed to organize our people. A general has to know how to lead and how to get his troops in the best position for battle. Walking your men off a cliff just because you're in charge is just stupid. I wanted to wait until we had enough weapons—so that if the Angels attacked, we would annihilate them.

Roger walked up and put his hand on one of the Hells Angels, in a friendly way, meaning to try to work things out. His intentions were good, but the way he went about it was completely ridiculous. He started to talk, but the Angels were not being very friendly. They were trying to provoke him. I stopped just off to the side, next to a slot machine, and looked around.

I saw that Cuete had positioned himself in front of the cashier's cage to my right. His buddy Shorty was not far away. Shorty is almost as dangerous as Cuete and usually carries two .45 pistols. If he had lived in the Old West, he would have been a fast gun. He doesn't like trouble, so he's the guy you go to when you've got a problem that the law can't fix. That night, he had given up only one of his pistols when Roger told everyone to stow their weapons. Another Mongol, nicknamed Bronson because he looked so much like the actor Charles Bronson, was a few feet to my left. There was nothing between us and the Angels except Roger.

Roger tried to make peace for about thirty seconds, but meanwhile a Hells Angel slipped around the corner of the little bar and karate-kicked a Mongol in the chest. Instantly all hell broke loose. The Angels brought their guns up and their knives out. They grabbed Roger and started stabbing him in the back, literally. He went down. I turned to get around behind the slot machine, and as I did, a Mongol who had been standing behind me pulled out his gun and returned fire. I could feel the wind of the bullet go past my ear, and I hunkered down fast. I figured that an Angel was gunning for me. They knew who I was.

Bullets suddenly were everywhere and it seemed to go forever, although it wasn't more than thirty or forty seconds. Bronson had been stabbed right away and was lying on the floor struggling. Shorty had been shot once and stabbed, but he had his gun out and was shooting back. Cuete had grabbed a stanchion beside the cashier's cage and was shot in the gut as soon as he picked it up. Five Angels chased one of our guys into an alcove and started beating the crap out of him. It all happened so fast that I wouldn't even know any of this if I hadn't later watched the tapes from the casino's security cameras.

Two Hells Angels and one Mongol, Bronson, died on the floor that night. It would have been a massacre if not for the few Mongols who had disobeyed Roger's orders.

Just about when everyone, even the ones with the guns, had scrambled for cover and the shooting had stopped, the police walked in. Hotel security had called them while the Angels were still massing. If Roger had waited two minutes, the police would have walked in and stopped the whole thing before it started. I didn't plan for that, but if he had waited another two minutes, Laughlin would never have happened.

The emergency medical people followed the police in. Thirteen people went to the hospital, including six Mongols, and nine of them were injured pretty badly. Some of them were airlifted to trauma centers. Somebody put Roger in a taxicab to a local hospital, and then he was flown to a medical center in Las Vegas. Cuete was sent to a hospital in Arizona. The hotel was locked down as soon as the shooting started, and the police separated everybody—Mongols in one room, Hells Angels in another, and witnesses in another—so that they could interview them and look at the casino videotapes of what had happened. No Mongols were arrested that night, but several Angels were.

Laughlin blew everything up. It just made a mess of things. First of all, we lost a good man and we had people seriously injured. There's pain there that will never completely go away. Ultimately, we were fighting because our club had entered their territory, but when it was all said and done, we were still in San Jose. What's the use in people dying for nothing? What did the Hells Angels gain by coming to our hotel?

Also, law enforcement now had something on video to prove to the public that the Mongols are animals. The police assume that we're criminals and dangerous to the public, but now they had head-line news to back them up. A lot of the early reports in the news-papers and elsewhere blamed the Mongols for starting the fight, as some did with Morongo. It was easy to jump to that conclusion be-cause it had all happened in our hotel.

The Las Vegas paper quoted the police as saying, "Intelligence reports indicated the Mongols intended to bolster their status by at-tacking members of the Hells Angels." Which was pure bullshit, but the average guy figures that we were all there itching for a fight, so when a few Hells Angels walked in, we jumped them. The paper made a big deal out of how it was the first multiple killing in a casino, at least since 1931. The whole prejudice against us just got backed up and fed on itself.

Of course the meeting with the heads of all the clubs just evapo-rated. It wasn't so much because there was violence, because motor-cycle clubs know that's something that can happen, but the whole atmosphere had been poisoned. The various other clubs started taking sides between us and the Angels, which just increased the animosity between everyone and the tension that was everywhere.

And there were the arrests and trials, which just went on and on and brought up all the same shit all over again. It took a year and a half for the Feds to hand down an indictment—against the Hells Angels. They had looked at the videotapes over and over, interviewed everybody who was on the scene, and decided that the Mongols had acted completely in self-defense.

But then everybody in Nevada got up in arms because there was this idea that we were the bad guys—nearby Arizona being a stronghold of the Hells Angels. So two years after the event, Nevada charged Shorty and Roger with murder. Can you believe that? Roger, after being stabbed several times, was supposed to have gotten up and attacked. It's just another example of why we think it's so hard to respect the justice system. Nevada also indicted the same seven Angels the Feds had indicted.

Three weeks later they added Curly, Pedro "Piper" Martinez, Walter "Bumper" Ramirez, and Benjamin "Secret" Leyva, along with another Hells Angel. Then in 2006, the Nevada Supreme Court threw out all the indictments on a technical issue and the state lawyers had to rewrite them. A few months after that, the Angels made a deal with prosecutors. Finally, five and half years after it all happened, Shorty agreed to a plea deal for shooting and killing the two Angels, and our other guys pleaded to various charges of battery. Even Roger. Curly actually had to plead guilty to firing his gun into a wall.

Of course, this was not only five years of disruption and having the papers rehash everything, it was also five years of bills for bail and for lawyers. Shorty's bail was six hundred thousand dollars, and the others were steep too. We got Shorty a top-drawer lawyer, not just a shyster. It all came out of our legal defense fund, which was something I started. Before that, you were on your own if you were arrested for something that happened because you were wearing your colors. I just thought it was the right thing to do. Here were guys who had defended the club, who really risked their lives for the club, so they deserved the best defense we could give them.

We asked everybody for more dues. Club dues can change depending on what the club needs that month or that year, but it's usually maybe five or ten or fifteen dollars a week. I can't tell you how proud I felt when it was time for us to defend our brothers in Laughlin and we asked these guys for three hundred dollars one month and four hundred dollars the next month, and on and on for months. Here are guys who are barely getting by and have families and work and still they come in and put their hard-earned money on the table. Some of our members are rich, but most of them just don't have much to spare. Didn't matter to those guys. You've got to love them, even if you disapprove of the way we live—these guys are amazing for sticking to what they believe and sticking to their word. With their money we put together a dream team of lawyers.

Then there were some losses that weren't really losses. After Laughlin, three people came up to me and said they didn't want to be in the club anymore. They didn't realize what could happen, they said, which just means they didn't realize what a Mongol is. I was glad. It was easy for them in the good times, but they couldn't take the tough times, so they're not really Mongols. Even worse were the guys who wanted to come back after the bad publicity had died down. I just said, "That's bullshit. Don't ever cross my path again."

Some of those losers are the ones you see on TV—behind a screen or a mask, with voices changed, complaining about me and the Mongols. I know who they are, and every single one of them has quit this club. They are angry at me because they think that maybe another national pres would be soft on them and let them back in. Some have gone to the Mexican mafia and told them how they can get me. Some have gone to law enforcement and given them all the information they can give about me. I know these things for a fact. They have tried every way they can to eliminate me in the hopes that someday they will be able to come back. As long as I have something to do with this club, those people will never, ever come back.

So Laughlin hurt us in just about every way imaginable, and I still wake up sometimes thinking what a waste it was and how it could have been avoided. And the more I think about it, the more I wonder why it wasn't avoided. If you think about it, it doesn't exactly add up. Here was a small town—literally a one-street town—that was crawling with law enforcement people of every kind. The minute we walked out of Harrah's Friday night, we were surrounded by cops, like a hundred of them. JC and I figured that the same thing was going on at the Flamingo. I mean there wasn't any way the cops would be able to stop two or three Hells Angels from slipping away and coming down to Harrah's, but I wasn't concerned about two or three.

In court, a local cop named Smitley said that after we went back to Harrah's, he went to talk to the Angels at the Flamingo and asked them to stay there all night. The Hells Angels leader, Smitley says, became indignant and said, "We have chosen a life of outlaws, we plan to live the life of outlaws, we don't need the police department, and we police ourselves. We don't care what the fuck you do, we're going to do what we have to do to protect ourselves." Did Lieutenant Smitley need any clearer signal that the Angels were looking for trouble? One of the cops with him said the Angels "were very aggressive. It was like they really didn't care that we were police officers doing our job."

Then there's something that I really don't understand. Harrah's not only had cameras inside, of course, they also had a camera outside focused on the entrance to the building. When you're watching the tape, you see some regular cars and people going in and out of the hotel, and some Mongols. Then you see a police car—actually a police jeep—drive by the entrance and pull into the parking lot. Five seconds later—the time is on the tape—the first of the Hells Angels pull up in front of Harrah's, flying their colors. Not just two or three of them, either, but five of them. And there are five more right behind them.

Of course, I don't ever depend on law enforcement to protect Mongols, I just wonder what they were doing. The cops in that jeep had to know that the Angels were behind them. Remember, you have to pull off the main street and go a ways down the driveway to get to the entrance to Harrah's. Why doesn't that jeep just stop at the front door?

At the trial, officers from the Las Vegas Gang Crimes Unit testified that they had seen the Hells Angels riding toward Harrah's in a big group and had rushed to the casino, "but trailed the bikers by about a minute." It's a mile and a half from the Flamingo to Harrah's. Why couldn't somebody radio ahead? Why didn't they warn the casino?

Not only that, we found out later that there were a couple of undercover cops who had infiltrated the Hells Angels at the Flamingo and they were around just when the first Angels were getting their gear ready to go to Harrah's.

But despite all this preparation and all those law enforcement bodies, thirty or forty Hells Angels were able to ride down on us with their weapons in their hands and start a gun battle. Can someone explain that to me?

No one ever hears about these details. What they remember is that the Mongols are a bunch of bloodthirsty killers. Can you blame me for saying that I'm proud of Shorty? That I'm proud of every brother who stood his ground in that casino in the face of many more armed Hells Angels and beat them? It's not the way I wanted it to happen, but now that it has happened, I can still say I'd rather have a Mongol on my side than anybody else.

10

A Place of Our Own

There were so many ripples from Laughlin, I couldn't have rested even if I wanted to. After it was all over, we all rode home together. It wasn't a coincidence, it was planned, but I had to give the members credit that they did what needed to be done even though they felt like shit.

There were several odd incidents after Laughlin that nobody can really explain. On the night of the shooting in Harrah's, about a half an hour after it started, a Hells Angel was killed on the road out of Laughlin. No one knows why. After Laughlin, several Hells Angels were killed in Arizona, at bars. Of course, even though we had nothing to do with any of these incidents, we were blamed for them. When I got back to L.A., I talked to Sonny Barger and George Christie, another Angel leader. Barger is pretty much retired now—he had throat cancer and moved to Arizona—but he and Christie have their influence. We were all going to try to work it out, that's all. There was no peace at hand.

A few weeks after Laughlin, Cuete was supposed to come back to Los Angeles, but we received intelligence that he would be assassinated on the highway on the way home. I was not going to take any chances with Cuete's life. He was still in intensive care, but he could be released to his family. I got in touch with his wife and we worked out a plan to escort him safely back to Los Angeles.

We borrowed a mobile home from a Mongol named Gramps and fixed it up so that Cuete could ride comfortably through the desert and south. I also found a registered nurse, Martha Flores, who would travel with us to make sure that Cuete would be all right during the trip.

I added one trick that I came up with from studying warfare. A mobile home is slow and sluggish, like a bomber. Bombers were always accompanied by fighter jets, which could maneuver around them and defend them from attack by other fighters. So I added a Camaro as an armed escort to the caravan. It would be able to zip around the mobile home and blast whoever tried to attack us.

Cuete's wife picked him up at the hospital in her own car, with several of us watching the whole time. But she only drove around the corner to where our mobile home was parked. We hustled him into it, made him secure, and took off for home. We were fully armed—rifles, shotguns, handguns, all legal—and every time a van pulled up next to us, we trained the weapons on that car. We alerted the driver to take evasive action if we saw a window start to roll down. At the first sight of a gun barrel in a car's window, we would have riddled the car with bullets. Luckily, no one tried to interfere with us. Cuete recovered completely.

After Laughlin, it was time for elections again. As we'd been doing for a couple of years, we rented a hall—we needed the space. Now that I had been named a national officer, I no longer needed anybody to run for me now—five-year rule be damned. As awful as Laughlin had been, I was more determined than ever to make the Mongols into the greatest motorcycle club in America. These guys deserved no less.

Roger hadn't been a real president since Laughlin anyway. Even after he had recovered from the stabbing, he hadn't been around, hadn't helped with the fund-raisers—hadn't even gone to them. Still, though, he was nominated. The club was furious that he had ordered the weapons put away at Laughlin and showed him no mercy. Out of hundreds of members, he received two votes, and one of them was his own. I have no idea who his buddy was—whoever nominated him, I guess—and that's probably a good thing. Sometimes my bad memory is a benefit to other people. I think Mike Munz nominated me, but it might have been JC. There was a kind of general uproar when it happened, so I don't recall exactly. JC was my national vice president.

Roger turned into kind of a sad story, but it was all his own doing. One very strict rule is that we don't fight other members during a meeting. I mean, we don't want to be fighting one another at any time, but these guys are pretty hardheaded, and I can't control them everywhere. In the meetings, I wanted peace. Roger had had a disagreement with another member, which started out as a verbal disagreement, but then one day in church I noticed that Roger looked different. He had his hair pulled back and he had that look, a look that I know very well, the look of someone who is going to fight. But before I could do anything about it, he approached the guy he had a problem with and sucker-punched him, wearing brass knuckles.

The brother bounced off a wall, but he's pretty tough and he proceeded to beat the shit out of Roger. When it was over, we discovered that Roger had broken another major club rule: he had brought a weapon into church. He had a big blade strapped to his ankle. He came in ready for battle against a brother.

But then he made it even worse. While we were waiting for the indictments to be handed down, some of the guys brought a suit against law enforcement and against Harrah's for allowing the fight to happen. Basically we were saying that they should have provided adequate security, prevented the Angels from coming into the hotel, and disarmed them. We weren't the only ones, either—some of the hotel guests filed the same kind of suit.

In any case, the club has a very strict rule that members never say who is in charge, either nationally or of a chapter. You do not name names to anybody, but to do it to law enforcement and in a court is a serious club offense. Roger Pinney went ahead and told them. Everyone was up in arms. In a general meeting the membership voted him out of the club. That is a very, very rare event, but it shows how mad they were. I intervened then, even though he'd been an idiot for so long. I felt that bad about taking his patch. Being a Mongol means so much to me that it is very, very hard for me to take that away from anyone, even Roger.

Now we had a real problem. This was a serious situation. Regardless of what an idiot Roger had been, it was hard for me to prospect an ex–national officer. It's like someone was the president of a company, but then was ousted and made to work as a janitor, cleaning up behind the workers. As much trouble as Roger had caused me, I personally didn't want to do it, and it would have looked bad for the club. It would just be an embarrassment. Finally, I told Roger that he should take some time off. "I don't want to see you picking up cans and bottles around the clubhouse. Instead of prospecting, I want you to stay away from the club for a year."

Roger thought this was a great deal. Unfortunately, he didn't know how to keep his mouth shut and how to go with the program while he was off. He started running down the club all over town, and of course making up stories about me and JC and others. He was complaining about the money members were contributing for the attorney fees, but he was one of the richest guys in the club. He didn't want to contribute, he complained when he did, and then his checks started bouncing. It turned into a real fiasco. The membership got tired of him and voted him out of the club. This time I wasn't going to overrule it.

knew that I had to make a lot of changes in the club and to the way people thought of us. After Morongo, after Laughlin, there was this idea that we were just animals. And criminals. We were dealing with the courts and the lawyers. The members who had quit were talking to reporters and doing their chickenshit anonymous appearances on the local news. One thing we did was to stay away from some of the runs that we normally would have participated in. A lot of people were still nervous that more fighting would happen if Mongols and Angels were in the same place at the same time, so we went to a lot of promoters and said that we would voluntarily stay away from events like the Ventura Beach Run, Palm Springs Bike Week, and the Hollister Run. Members were disappointed, but we needed to put some distance between Laughlin and the Mongols in public.

The cops were hassling us more than ever, and I have to say that I found what they were doing really frustrating and idiotic. I had learned from San Jose that image could make a big difference, and I was working very hard on changing the club's image, and the reality too, but what law enforcement was doing was dragging me down. Let me give you an example.

I was constantly encouraging the members to get jobs. I want them to have jobs because then they can pay their dues and fix their motorcycles up, and they aren't tempted to make money by stealing or by selling drugs. The courts agree—that's what they say to you when they release you. When you're on parole or probation, getting a job is one of the best things you can do, for obvious reasons. The courts consider that if you're employed you're keeping busy, contributing to society—which is true. One time, John Ciccone, the AFT agent, said to me, "Doc, if you could keep your guys from hitting the street and fighting with everybody we wouldn't have all these problems." You would think they would be happy that our guys are getting jobs.

But they aren't. They actually pursue us on the job. The police will call up the place you work, say a tow-truck company, which is basically dependent on the business the police give them, and say, "Do you realize you have a guy who is a part of a criminal organization?" That is, the Mongols. If the owner of the company doesn't do anything, some other cops will make the same call: "Why are you hiring members of a criminal organization?" Never mind that maybe the member has never been arrested. Never mind that he may be an excellent tow-truck driver. After the police lean on you two or three times and hint they can make or break your business, you fire that Mongol. We get guys who have lost their jobs over that stuff. Luckily there are owners who really know us and just say that the guy is a good employee who never did anything wrong. But I don't understand this at all, except I have to think that this is the personality of these police—if you are their enemy for some reason, they will do anything to hurt you, whether it's good for society or not.

I also tried to cut down on the kinds of situations that would make the members get into fights. For instance, after Laughlin, a lot of other small clubs were stupid enough to try to put on the California rocker that we had fought so hard to wear. My members would go somewhere and run across someone wearing a California rocker. Naturally, being Mongols, they would walk up to the person and say, "Hey, you're not supposed to wear that." The other person would call law enforcement, and the next thing you know there was a fight and one of my guys would be in jail. I was tired of the violence over that rocker. I didn't want it anymore, so I said, "Let's stop fighting for this thing. It doesn't mean that much anymore. The bottom line is, we are so well known already that nothing can tarnish our image. We don't have to show who we are by showing that California rocker."

I just felt that my members were worth a lot more than the exclusive right to wear the rocker. I'm so proud of these guys and I love them so much that it really hurts me when they get arrested for this kind of stupidity. "I'm tired of you guys going to jail," I yelled at them, "because you beat up some idiot who doesn't have enough sense to know that he shouldn't be wearing that and thinks he's Mr. John Wayne."

I really felt that something needed to be done, and of course Laughlin was still on my mind, and I thought I could put the two together. So I wrote a full-page magazine ad—just words, no pictures—that was basically a call for peace. It said that we regretted what happened in Laughlin, and it apologized to the innocent bystanders who were caught in it, but it also said that we believed in our right to defend ourselves. It laid out some of what went down in Laughlin and pointed out that many in the public questioned how law enforcement could have been so incompetent. It said that we had been working with other clubs to prevent problems like Laughlin before they happened. The last paragraph said:

> As further proof that we are sincere in this quest for peace, we
> are granting the following request. For over thirty years, the only
> two clubs that have earned the right to wear "California" on their

bottom rocker have been the Mongols and the Hells Angels. This still holds true today. In a gesture of pure generosity and good faith, we, the Mongols, are granting permission to any and all presently existing clubs in California, including the Hessians, Rare Breed, Vagos, Sundowners, all law enforcement clubs, etc. to wear the "California" bottom rocker. Enjoy, but never forget the price paid by those who earned it.

No one wanted to print this ad. I don't know if it was just because we were the Mongols or just because we were largely Hispanic or what. Finally a magazine named *Hot Bike* agreed to print it at its usual rates. No one in the club complained because they trusted me. Everyone in the biker world knew the history.

Women were another reason that we had a bad image. In the biker world, in most of the clubs, a woman is property, and the Mongols were as bad as anybody. Members beat up their wives or girlfriends too often. To me, it was just wrong. Women shouldn't be treated that way. Domestic violence was just a drag on everybody. But I had to give them a reason that worked for them. I would argue that it was a waste of their time. If they beat up their old lady, they could go to jail for six months or a year, and for what? Go to anger management, I told them, like I was only concerned about them and not the poor woman who was getting hell.

People are always pointing to the fact that the women wear jackets that say "Property of So-and-so." To the outside world, this means that we make women into slaves and treat them like—well, like property. That would be true in the everyday suburban world, but in this world, "property of" gives the woman a feeling of security. She's telling the world she is with so-and-so and nobody had better mess with her—because so-and-so will kick the shit out of anybody who does. The women want those "property of" jackets as much as the guys do. We have a club rule that you cannot take a woman away from another member—at least not without his permission—and that's another rule that is strictly enforced.

It's funny, one of the first times I noticed a problem about women and Mongols was at a club in Santa Monica with Money and some of the other guys and their wives. This was when I had just become a Mongol. Money had a couple of real knock-out women with him who dressed very provocatively. If you were a man, it was hard to keep your eyes off these women. I think if you were a woman, it was hard, because the wives of some of the other members started to get really furious and began to bitch at the girls. I managed to cool things down, but I learned that the women could be just as much of a danger as the Mongols. So every Mongol is responsible for making sure that the women he brings to our parties know how to behave.

Another thing I insisted on was getting rid of the swastikas, which is another thing you see all over the biker world that makes people think we are just filled with hate and brutality. When I outlawed the swastika, some of the white brothers came to me and complained that the Hispanics had Mexican flag tattoos and things like that on their vests. "Well, I love my white brothers," I said, "but there has to be something else that will represent them better than a swastika. A swastika is not a symbol of whites, it's a hate symbol."

Some of the members were surprised to hear this, which shows you that the problem is not always hate. Sometimes it's just ignorance. I know this because when I was growing up, if people wanted to say that a certain person was a real tightwad with money, they called him a Jew. I grew up thinking that "Jew" was a synonym for a penny-pincher. I had no idea it had anything to do with someone's religion. I really wasn't prejudiced, but I was ignorant. A lot of these guys didn't know the swastika meant the Nazis and World War II and the extermination of millions of Jews.

Some members were so stuck on the swastika that I had to go to the arguments about self-interest again. I said to them, "Don't be stupid. Many of the judges and many of the district attorneys in Los Angeles are of the Jewish faith." I remembered going to the hospital to visit Red Dog after he'd been hurt in a motorcycle accident. He wasn't wearing a shirt when I walked in and there was that big swastika on his chest. Since I was in the medical world for my regular job, I knew that a lot of the doctors in the hospital were Jewish, and I thought to myself, *I wonder what these docs think about this guy.* "Some of you guys are going to get shot," I'd say to the club, "or be in a wreck or something, and if you get a doctor of the Jewish faith, he's not going to feel very good about seeing that swastika. I mean he will do his job, but he may not go out of his way to make you comfortable."

So instead of just saying it was wrong and insulting and hurt a lot of people needlessly, I had to make it seem that I was only concerned about them. Some of them saw the logic in it and took off the swastikas. We literally had to strip some of these guys—actually take their vest and cut the swastika off it. There wasn't anything we could do about the tattoos. We'd ask them to cover them up somehow.

Some of the guys said things like, "This was given to me by a Mongol twenty years ago and he has passed on." I'd say, "Well, take it home and put it in your drawer." I just made it very clear that we are not a hate group and we especially have nothing to do with a swastika or the SS lightning bolts, which were also very common. We still have to watch. Once in a while one of the very old members will try to sneak a little swastika pin on, and we'll take it from him. I haven't seen anyone wearing one for a long time now—they were mostly on some of the older white members and they have either retired or died.

But not everything I did was a pain in the ass for everybody. I decided that the Mongols needed a clubhouse, a place where we could meet and throw parties. It would be useful as a recruiting tool too. I also wanted to get individual packs of Mongols off the street. Too often members were going to clubs in threes and fours and they'd start mixing with the public, which led to fights. Very often, civilians sitting in a bar would see a Mongol and decide that he didn't look so tough after all. That usually led to trouble. And I would lose a Mongol to jail or to death.

So I gave everybody the assignment of submitting two or three addresses of a potential clubhouse each month. You need a location where you're not bothering anybody, so it can't be in a residential area. There has to be parking and freeway access so we don't have to ride through a quiet neighborhood. It had to be a building big enough to hold everybody. Finally somebody submitted the name of a place in the city of Whittier, in an industrial area. As soon as I walked into the place with JC, I could picture where the bar would be, where the pool tables would be, everything. Most clubhouses are just homes that people fix up to have parties in, but this was a huge warehouse—lots of room for everything. I went to the rental agent and told them we were a group of motorcycle enthusiasts who needed a place where we could show motorcycles, have bike shows, and repair bikes, all of which was perfectly true. We leased it.

It was a hell of a lot of work. We painted, we built offices, we built the bar. They thought I was crazy when I said, "I want you to go and find me three old-fashioned bathtubs for behind the bar to put the beer in," but they did it. And when we were all done it was exactly as I pictured it the day I walked in. The clubhouse was open Thursday through Sunday, and we paid the monthly rent and electricity and such out of dues, but you didn't have to pay to get in. We would just assign each member a portion of the rent as "clubhouse dues" separate from his regular dues. After a while we started keeping receipt books that listed all the members in the area and showed how much everybody had paid every month toward the rent and upkeep—maybe forty dollars, depending on what we were doing at the club that month.

One thing I was very happy about was that Little Rubes really took charge of the club. JC had nominated him for membership after Laughlin, and since he had been around the club as long as I had, and had put himself in the crossfire at Laughlin and done everything else a Mongol could do, he was quickly accepted. He didn't have to prospect, but that was not because he was my son, it was because he had already shown that he was a Mongol.

Little Rubes had taken a few college courses, but just about the time we found the clubhouse, he started working for a security company. Then one night I couldn't be at the club and Little Rubes said, "Go on, go to work. I'll take care of things." So he filled in that night and never left. And he started to organize things right away. So he was always around the clubhouse and people would call with questions about the club, or who should they call if they needed to bail somebody out—really just everything. Pretty soon he was so good at answering the questions that we made him a national sergeant at arms.

At first everybody would bring what they wanted to drink and we would give them a ticket for it. If you brought in four cases of Corona, you would get ninety-six tickets stamped "Corona." We had refrigerators, ice makers, and everything else you needed. But this was another case when law enforcement began working against what seems to me like a good thing for society. They made every step of the process difficult. For instance, very quickly we started getting threats from law enforcement to close us down. They said they didn't believe that the tickets were just about drinks. So we changed the policy. Members just brought in what they wanted to drink for the night. We provided everything else—glasses, setups, ice, and what have you. The only problem with that was there were a lot of ice buckets and ice chests and water leakage to deal with, but we made do.

We were ideal tenants for the landlords. We were only there Thursday through Sunday and only at night. All the businesses in that area were able to use our parking lot during the day. We didn't manufacture anything so we didn't have a lot of trash to pick up. We cleaned up after ourselves. It was like we were ghosts; they never saw us there.

There were some great parties there, good times. Each chapter could have a weekend, and we had birthday parties, fund-raisers, bike shows, combination car and bike shows, just all kinds of terrific events. At first I had to reinforce some of the rules. I told the members, "All you have to do is beat up one guy in the middle of these parties and people are going to be terrified again. That will just reinforce their idea that we're animals.

"I never want to see anybody get socked up, never want to see a women abused in here. Not only are they people, but they wouldn't be here if they weren't friendly toward us. Why would you want to abuse them? Why would you want to mistreat them? If a woman drinks too much and passes out, she will wake up not only with her watch and ring, but with her pants on and everything else. No exceptions." Some of the old-timers made comments that women were running the club now, but it was more political than actually arguing the point. They were just mad that the club had changed.

I've never really ever had a serious relationship with a woman, though I've had a great many women in my life. I've moved too fast, been in too much danger for me ever to feel very comfortable with a wife or a steady girlfriend. But that doesn't mean I don't want female companions in my life. And I wanted them to be able to party with me. But at first I would ask women to a Mongol party and they would say that they heard that Mongols rape women, or Mongols beat women up, and the like. But after a few years, women were asking, even pleading, to be invited to our parties. I would go to work at the hospital and somebody would find out who I was and say, "My cousin wants to go to one of those parties but she doesn't know anybody who will ask her. Please, can you help?" It actually became some kind of a privilege to go to our parties among women, even young and pretty ones. I felt like I'd accomplished something there.

Of course, the police fought that too. The cops would stand around outside the club and stop the women as they walked into the party in their miniskirts and high heels. "You're not going in there, are you?" they'd say. "Those guys are a bunch of rapists and thugs." Personally I think it was jealousy. They were working and the terrible Mongols had all these cute young girls coming to party with them. I couldn't help but remember the old days when there were no women within a mile of a Mongol. And that to new Mongols, this was the only life they knew. They would say, "This is cool—these guys aren't afraid of anything, they've got women like rock stars do, and they have awesome bikes. I want to be a Mongol."

The cops did everything they could to shut us down. They called the landlords and said that we were a criminal organization. We had to pay ahead of time, and in cash, and keep our area cleaner than anybody else. I would watch outside in the middle of the night for the graffiti artists. I would stop them and say, "Look buddy, this is the Mongols' clubhouse, and we don't want you to be writing on our walls." They found another wall. I didn't have to tell anyone twice.

The police raided the club for drugs and illegal weapons and anything else they could think of. They never found anything. Finally, I guess they were really frustrated, because they drove some kind of small tank through the wrought-iron doors at about four or five in the morning on a weekday. They just destroyed the front of the building. They searched the clubhouse and didn't find a thing. They walked away more frustrated than ever. The head detective said to me, "How did you know we were coming?" Of course they wanted to believe that we had found out ahead of time and taken away all the incriminating evidence. They must think we are total morons if they think we would have this very public Mongol place and fill it up every day with stolen bikes, illegal drugs, and machine guns.

When it happened, the management called JC and he called me because I was the closest to the clubhouse. When I went down there, the police were still in there, wandering around, trying to find something that would make the raid worth it. They took all the money out of the cash drawer and we never got it back. They also took the receipt books.

But the police still weren't done with that clubhouse. We received a letter from the management of the building saying that the police had found stolen motorcycles and illegal weapons. It was a lie, pure and simple. But it was the last straw for the management. They could see that the police were not going to quit bothering them until the Mongols were back out on the street again. The police basically got us kicked out of there.

We went to court to fight to get our money back, but they said we would have to prove that it wasn't drug money. Unless we could do that, they would keep the money as evidence. So we asked them to bring in the receipt books, which show that the money that they took was about equal to the total of the clubhouse dues, and that each member had contributed a small sum. But in court the police said the receipt books didn't exist. They didn't try to explain what happened to them, because according to them they had never existed in the first place. It was just another outright lie, and the judge saw through it and ordered them to return the money. Two years later, I'm still waiting to see it.

What I don't understand is how they can do things like that and have a clear conscience. I put up a clubhouse to prevent my Mongols from fighting civilians, but the police helped shut it down and then took the money that we had worked for and the receipt books and then they lost the receipt books in order to accuse us of dealing drugs.

Think about that. We lost a month's rent and paid thousands of dollars to repair the door and the wall of the building. Is it any wonder that Mongols don't respect law enforcement? There is no winning with these guys, and what they're doing to us has nothing to do with preventing crime. If you drive by that building now it's covered with graffiti, and the neighborhood looks like a ghetto. The only reason I didn't have an uprising among my brothers is that they are so used to the police giving them grief. They suck it up and keep their stoneface. They are warriors, and tough ones. We needed that, because we were just about to face an enemy much stronger than either the Hells Angels or the police.

11

A Two-Front War

ne of the things that I have learned most completely from my experience with the Mongols is that nothing is more dangerous than success. The Mongols were growing so rapidly that it was hard to keep track of it—we were heading toward a thousand members by the time the police·raided my house in 2004. The few we had lost after Laughlin had long since been replaced by new recruits who were much better Mongols than the ones who were still sniping at me. We had chapters all over the country.

But the bigger we became, the more worried the Hells Angels were that we would take over from them as the biggest, baddest club in California. Not that we cared. The bigger we became, the more the police wanted to catch us doing all those things they fantasized we were doing with guns and drugs and vehicles. Not that we cared.

The bigger we became, the more local news dispensed comic-book stories about us being rapists and murderers. Not that we cared. All because we were a huge success.

What is kind of ironic is that even the criminals started to believe the stories. We know that the Hells Angels tried to form alliances with the Mexican mafia and with the Nuestra Familia, the Northern California Hispanic gangs, since they couldn't take us on their own, but they refused. The Mexican mafia began to believe that we must have huge amounts of money, since there were now so many Mongols and—in this they thought the same way as the police—we must be dealing drugs or doing something else illegal. It's even more ironic that we—always known as a Hispanic motorcycle club— should be targeted by a group that was created to defend Hispanics.

The incident that kicked off the confrontation involved some Mongols who were partying in a Motel 6 in San Gabriel. Now, motels are very often used as places to manufacture or package drugs for a drug deal. If you're a drug dealer, you can go to a motel that's not one of your usual places and the police can't find you easily, as long as you don't attract attention to yourself. You give the motel a false name and address, if they ask, and once you're finished, you just walk away. Neat and clean. However, especially when you are working with La eMe, you never call attention to yourself. You have to give up any kind of gangbanging so that you don't get caught with the drugs.

In this one incident, a small-time drug manufacturer was doing his business in the Motel 6, but for some reason, he wasn't smart about following the rules and got into an argument with the Mongol who was partying there. He shot the Mongol and killed him, and that led to a real shoot-out. The Mongols riddled his truck with bullets, so to get away he crashed through a fence, slid down an embankment, and landed on the freeway. The police noticed this truck with the lights shot out and the bullet holes and stopped him. Eventually they connected him with the murder at the Motel 6.

Not too long after that, Cuete came to me and said that he had been approached by a member of the Mexican mafia, an individual known as Dumbo. I knew Dumbo. One time he got into a jam in Arizona and he called me up to ask if the Mongols could help him out with some backup. He called me because we reach out to more places than La eMe can. I did him that favor.

Dumbo said La eMe wanted to speak with us about problems our club was having with their members. We had expected this. Cuete and I both knew what was going to happen: they were going to ask us for money and we were going to refuse.

Cuete and I set up the meeting at a bike shop at the corner of Washington and Sorenson in Whittier. The bike shop was closed during our meeting so no civilians would be around. The shop had two entrances: one regular door and a large bay of roll-up doors. Cuete and I came early and we were sitting in the showroom when a Ford Bronco pulled up. I could see the driver was a very large, heavyset woman, and the passenger was Dumbo, who jumped out as the woman parked the car.

Dumbo came in and we sat down at a small round table in the showroom, the kind of table you might see at a bar with stools around it. His eyes looked glassy to me, and you could tell that he was not in his right mind. You could also tell that he was a real lowlife. He started to blather, but his basic point was that they wanted us to start paying taxes. The Mexican mafia extorts money, which they call taxes, from drug dealers and certain businesses throughout California. They divide the state into different areas and each area has a tax collector. I objected that the Mongols did not deal drugs, like most of the people they tax, but he said he didn't care about that. The Mongols were getting big, he said, so they should be able to pay a tax.

We would never allow this to happen to us, but we let Dumbo ramble on until it became clear that he was also trying to double-cross his own people. He offered to cut the amount of the tax money if we gave him something personally—money and maybe a couple of motorcycles. Now I knew we had a real problem. Not because I was afraid of Dumbo or the mafia, but just because dealing with these individuals is difficult to begin with—and dealing with someone who is double-crossing his own people is extra difficult. I was angry already that he had the nerve to ask the Mongols for taxes, but to ask for a bribe as well meant that he was contemptible. We would never pay anybody just to survive, but at least we should be able to deal with someone who had some honor.

Not only all that, but then he said that in return for us paying taxes we would be able to go out and gangbang against anybody we wanted to. This is when I knew that he was not dealing with reality, because first, we were not interested in gangbanging at all, and second, we would defend ourselves and enforce justice whenever and wherever we wanted to anyway.

So he was sitting there, mumbling about us paying taxes, and I let him talk because he was clearly more of a danger to himself than to me, and the more he talked the more he was hanging himself. He topped it all off by making me an offer. He said that if I personally agreed to the tax but the club turned the idea down, I would basically have the keys to the system. That meant that if I was ever arrested, I would have no problems while I was locked up. This infuriated me even more. He had now offended me by demanding taxes, disgusted me by asking for a bribe, and insulted me by suggesting that I would sell out my club.

I was so angry I went right back in my head to my gangbanging days. I had a .38-caliber handgun in my pocket, and I kept thinking how easy it would be to put a bullet in his forehead. At one point, he asked to go to the bathroom. He was so confident that no one would hurt a representative of La eMe that he didn't think for a moment that he was in the least bit of danger.

While he was in the bathroom, I opened the door and looked out back. The woman was waiting in the Bronco. I walked over to the bay doors and started measuring them with my hands and looking at some of the equipment that was blocking the way. Cuete immediately realized what I was doing and came up to me and said, "Look, we can't do anything right now. I gave my word that he would leave here alive." Cuete's word was important, so I gave up on planning. To be honest, I didn't want to have to deal with carrying around his girlfriend's body, since she would have to go too.

Still, something had to be done. These guys are nothing but 'hood monkeys, which meant they had no idea what they were getting into and they were going to cause problems for me. For instance, my phones are tapped by the Feds. These guys were going to start calling me and talking their stupidity for the cops to record. I'll give you an example of why this would be a problem for me. The national president of the Bandidos was indicted, and they threatened to put him away for life because of something he said on the telephone. Now this is an older guy, fairly wealthy, who owns a Harley dealership in Washington. He would never order anything illegal; it's not in his interest.

But younger members of the club had called him from time to time because federal agents had come knocking, and George would say, "Don't tell them anything. You don't have to talk to them." That is interfering with a federal witness. I know it sounds ridiculous, but I've been there. They indicted him on pure phone conversations. What they wanted to prove is that he was a head guy of a criminal organization and here he is telling his members to not cooperate with the authorities. They were trying to put him away for life, and although they didn't succeed, he did do some time.

So the police would use anything this lowlife said and find a way to make me responsible for it or involved in it, and everyone would end up in prison. I even told Dumbo when he came back from the head that the Mongols wouldn't give him anything, that I wouldn't give him anything, and that this was not leading anywhere but to prison, for everyone involved. This guy paid no attention. This guy was nothing more than a straight-out 'hood monkey. He couldn't even imagine what he was getting into.

A week or two later Cuete told me Dumbo wanted a second meeting. It would have been disrespectful of me to refuse, but I didn't want this to go on and on. This time Dumbo was a little more scared than the first time because he set up a meeting at a public place—a Denny's. Once again he was glassy-eyed, once again he went through the routine about the taxes and the double-cross, and once again I told him that it was not going to happen. The only thing different was that this time he talked about what would happen to us inside the prison system if we didn't coop-erate. That only made me mad all over again. Taxes were for weaklings. Cuete was losing his patience with this guy too, so we walked out.

It just so happened that we were having one of our semiannual membership meetings at that time, and four or five hundred of us would be at a hotel meeting room to discuss club business. I felt it was important for the club to know what was going on, because I knew this was about to get ugly. I stood up on the platform and looked at four or five hundred faces, with their shaved heads or their ponytails and their mustaches and their tattoos. They knew what it meant when the Mexican mafia made a demand on you. They knew that blood was in the air. Every last one of them said, "There is no fucking way." I knew that was going to be their answer, but seeing all these guys standing shoulder to shoulder and saying, "Not one fucking dollar" really made me very proud. *Now,* I thought grimly, *let the games begin.*

A week later Cuete told me Dumbo wanted us to meet with some different individuals from the Mexican mafia, but the club thought it was becoming too risky for me to go to these meetings. The people from La eMe picked a restaurant named Taco Boy in Pico Rivera, on the corner of Rosemead and Slauson, for the meeting, and they said they wanted no more than three people on each side. Cuete took another member, Happy, who is also very respected in our club, and then we were assisted by a special representative. A very high ranking member from the Mexican mafia, someone in Pelican Bay, had heard about these meetings and decided it was not the way the Mongols should be treated, so he sent a representative to go along with Cuete and Happy. There are factions even within La eMe, and sometimes they will wind up working at cross-purposes. They even had a disagreement at the table with the special rep. That was very unusual and did not speak well for Dumbo.

When meetings like this go on we are always concerned for our people's safety, and one of the things we do to make sure things go somewhat in our favor is to have a response team standing by. A response team is very similar to a police SWAT team and is fully armed. If a meeting starts to get ugly, the response team's first responsibility is to save our people. If it's too late to do that, they'll make sure that no one from the other side survives, to send a message that we will not be bullied. That day, our response team consisted of nine people, me among them. I would not allow others to risk their lives without risking mine. We had four vehicles, AK-47s, and walkie-talkies.

When Cuete, Happy, and the representative of La eMe walked into the Taco Boy, there were maybe forty individuals waiting for them—some in the restaurant, some outside in the alley, and some in the parking lot. Things immediately began to get heated. Cuete got on his radio and warned me. We immediately jumped into the vehicles and rolled. Picture four vehicles going down the road, the passengers wearing ski masks and holding AK-47s. It could have been Beirut. In a situation like that, you do not stop for anything. If law enforcement gets in the way, you move them.

When we were one block from the Taco Boy, I noticed there was a van with two people in it parked at a public-storage-business lot. As we passed, they started to talk into a radio. They were clearly surveillance. I pulled up my AK-47 and I pointed it at the van just when the radio crackled. Cuete yelled, "You've been seen, you've been seen! Stand down!" Apparently one of the lookouts had run into the restaurant screaming, "The Mongols are surrounding us! The Mongols are surrounding us!" He said that the people in the Taco Boy were panicking, so it would be a full-scale battle if we rode up. I could hear people screaming in the background over his two-way radio.

I trusted Cuete, so we pulled off our ski masks, put our guns down, and drove into a Jim's Burgers down the street. Everybody ordered food and acted like regular customers, though we were ready to pick up the weapons and run to Taco Boy if something happened. In fact, Cuete somehow got everyone calmed down, and the meeting went on as scheduled, but it was still the same bullshit. Nothing was agreed on, but they showed terrible disrespect in lying about the number of their people at the meeting and misrepresenting what La eMe was offering, especially in front of a representative of La eMe itself.

It was about this time that I came out of work one day to find ATF agent John Ciccone and a special sheriff's deputy working on La eMe sitting on my truck. They showed respect, at least, by not barging into the hospital. "We have to warn you, Ruben," Ciccone said, "that there is a contract out on you, from Pelican Bay." I guess he thought this would make me afraid, or make me ask for his help or something like that. At least he thought it was worth a try. I told him that I was aware of the situation.

Things went from bad to worse. For the next month or so, there were shoot-outs. Some of their guys were shot, and a Mongol was hit in the leg. One day about fifteen Mongols were riding up the freeway through the Montebello area and a black SUV came down the on-ramp, a window dropped, and shots blazed out at the Mongols.

Cuete was in the pack, and as usual, he kept his cool. He pulled up next to the pack and signaled them to evade and escape. Instantly the bikes scrambled through the different lanes at a speed no car can match. They were quickly out of range. Cuete, however, saw a construction area and pulled his bike over as the rest of the pack went by him. This was at the junction of the 57 freeway and 60. Because La eMe was at war with us, he was carrying a fully automatic TEC-9. He hid behind one of the construction barriers, and as the SUV came speeding up the freeway, he stepped out into the slow lane.

You can imagine that these guys were surprised to see someone they'd just shot at standing in the freeway, and before they could react, he let go a burst into their front windshield. They were lucky. The vehicle screeched to a stop and went into reverse at top speed. When they were out of range, Cuete put the handgun back in his waistband and took off on his bike. He later complained to me that he burned himself in the groin because the barrel of the gun was red hot.

That kind of craziness went on for a while. Then I got a message that the other side wanted to work something out. I said, "No problem." They suggested we meet at Camacho's Cantina at Universal CityWalk, six people on each side. I had learned from the last meeting. I had six Mongols at the table, but maybe twenty-five dressed like tourists walking around outside, taking pictures. I myself had a hand grenade in my pocket, and I wasn't the only one. I was glad that the restaurant was empty when Dumbo and his crew walked in.

This time they said that they wanted thirty-five thousand dollars a month in taxes. I had to laugh; I really couldn't hold it in anymore. I basically told them, "Fuck you and don't bother me anymore. I'm not giving you a single fucking dollar." That was the same as declaring all-out war.

It was hard times. Every weekend brought another shooting. The news media, particularly in Southern California, jumped all over the story. My name and my face were on TV every night. The owner of a tattoo shop, not a Mongol, was killed. Many people said he was shot because he employed a Mongol, but actually he had refused to pay tax to La eMe a few weeks before. It makes me extremely proud that while everyone around us was terrified, the club went on with business as usual. At the beginning of the problem, a dozen members dropped their colors. They didn't come to me, because they knew what I would think of them. It was just as well, and the club was still growing anyway.

Now that we were at war with the Hells Angels and the Mexican mafia, the club became really concerned about my safety. La eMe has its methods, but the Hells Angels are known for using dynamite. The club started checking under my car for dynamite with these mirrors on arms that extended under the car. One day they found several sticks wired to the underside of the car. That was when Little Rubes decided he was personally going to supervise my security. He brought in his friend Chickie, who works at the same security company, to help. They were all over this. I had a bodyguard around me at all times and layers of security in front of and behind me. It was airtight. I was in Palm Springs once and I heard someone say, "The president doesn't even get that kind of security."

One of the Hells Angels' tricks is simply to drive by your house at night and throw dynamite through your window. So Rubes decided to chicken-wire my house. They stretched chicken wire across the windows, because the dynamite will bounce off the wire into the yard. You're much more likely to survive that. They would also check under my car every morning to make sure no one had wired dynamite under it. I started to make it a habit to leave the door open when I got into my car and to keep one foot out on the pavement. Then if the car blew up, I would be thrown to the side. I hadn't done that since back in the old days.

One day I got a call to go to a Mongol's house. When I got there I was happy to see some of our members from other states, but I also thought there must be some big trouble in the works. If no one had told me that these guys were coming, it was because they didn't want to leave any messages that might be traced. These guys were explosives experts. They lived in very rural areas, and one of their pastimes was to build shacks in their backyards and blow them up. They told me they knew we were in a war and wanted to contribute their services.

That was okay with me except if they blew a guy's house up, it wouldn't be just the enemy in it—there could be wives, children, pets, grandparents, friends. So far we had managed to keep families out of it, and I wanted it to stay that way. Even if the other guys were out to kill Mongols, I didn't want to retaliate against their innocent family members. So I emphasized over and over again, no explosives—it had to stay between La eMe and the Mongols.

We have a very large intelligence network, and it was working very hard to track down Dumbo and his crew. We found out that Dumbo was riding a Japanese motorcycle that he had taxed someone for. We obtained a complete description of that bike and of Dumbo's hangouts. We made some inquiries of girls he had dated in the area. He and his crew were constantly on the move, staying in different hotels almost every night. At one point we came extremely close to catching up with him when he was staying at the Disneyland Hotel in Anaheim. He left the room minutes before we got there.

During the war with La eMe, I realized that my life is what other people think of as a nightmare. I was working on my lawn one day, and a sheriff's car drove up. The cop inside looked out at me, and said, "What are you going to do, Doc?"

"Do about what?" I asked. I was really mystified as to what this cop was talking about. I was a little suspicious.

"About La eMe," he said, and I could see that he was really concerned. "Those are really bad guys, Doc. They kill people for breakfast."

I almost laughed at him, I was so disgusted. This guy really thought I would be afraid of this. It's just part of my life.

Throughout this time, my members never let me down. I was having a "special construction" Harley made—a bike that was built from scratch, without a single factory part. It was built by a Mongol named Knuckles, who was president of the Orange County chapter. The front wheel and suspension were raked forward, and the back end was a softail. The engine was a 100-inch RevTech; it had a six-speed transmission with overdrive and an oversized rear tire. Even the saddle was custom made, hand tooled to perfection.

The gas tank and fenders were painted by a young guy from East L.A., Hector of Kustom Kare. As a surprise gift to me, the club picked it up and had another artist airbrush a smoking shotgun barrel and one of my favorite lines, modified a bit by me:

> *I don't apologize*
> *For the way*
> *I've lived my life*
> *And I refuse*
> *To be a fool*

Dancing on a
String held by
All those so-
Called big shots.
I don't apologize, that's my life.

These are Vito Corleone's words, from *The Godfather.*

I was being approached from all sides by people who wanted to join the Mongols to fight La eMe, but I turned most of them away. I didn't want the fighting to increase, but to die down. I thought that the whole problem was because of a few individuals who had absolutely no sense. Our relationship with La eMe had been very good before, and I was sure that the war would end sooner or later.

It did. Just as I'd predicted, Dumbo wound up in prison because of his own stupidity—he said something on the phone while the law was listening in. He and his crew were all arrested and wound up in prison. Then while they were inside, La eMe discovered that Dumbo had been trying to cheat the organization. At the meeting at Camacho's, he was supposed to ask me for a one-time payment of thirty-five thousand dollars, not thirty-five thousand a month. That is what he'd been instructed to ask for—not that we would have agreed.

His superiors were very upset at his treachery. Consequently, Dumbo was stabbed on two occasions while he was locked up. He survived them both and he was now under protective custody in the county jail system.

Eventually the war with La eMe wound down. One of their people contacted me and said there was no need, it was all based on misunderstandings. "We are all Hispanics," he said. "Why are we fighting each other?"

Something Rotten

f you're interested in motorcycle clubs at all, you've probably heard about a book by an undercover cop, William Queen, who called himself Billy St. John when he was in the Mongols. The cover of his book calls the Mongols "America's Most Violent Outlaw Motorcycle Gang," and he's made a little career of talking about us and doing publicity for his book, *Under and Alone,* ever since it was published in 2005. That makes it seem like he's talking about things that happened recently. Actually, Queen started working undercover in March 1998 and got out of it in May 2000, just about the time that I was starting to have some influence in the Mongols but before I had any kind of official position. I don't mean to say that I wasn't part of the club then, but I think that in the last eight years a lot has changed, and Billy Queen doesn't know anything about it. He's still getting information from his friends in the Bureau of Alcohol, Tobacco, Firearms and Explosives, but it's all from their point of view.

Of course if you want to believe his story from top to bottom, I won't be able to change your mind. Many people want to believe anything that a law enforcement officer, or former officer, says, especially when it's published in a book. Like I said at the beginning of this book, I can only ask that you ride with me for a while and look at things from my side with an open mind. By the way, I did not start writing this book because of William Queen's book. Several people suggested to me that I should write a book, but it was not something I imagined doing. However, now that I have the chance, I will offer some different perspectives on William Queen and his version of the events.

I should say first that there is nothing you could tell me about the San Fernando Valley chapter that I would defend or say didn't, or at least couldn't, happen. That chapter was filled with the kind of guys I didn't want in the club. These guys Rocky and Easy were just despicable characters. I disciplined Domingo and Evel for what they did during that time, and they have straightened out. That whole group out there lived the old ways, not the way we live now. It was difficult for them to recruit, so they wound up with members who were the pits. They were a group that even we didn't hang with—they were bullies and they did a lot of stupid shit.

The chapter was filled with poor leadership and poor judgment and poor individuals. Red Dog was one of the regulars there, and I think that was because he felt comfortable with guys who liked to do drugs and were generally screwups. He could take advantage of them. I have said that Red Dog needed money to buy drugs, and he made a lot of money from that chapter. He brought in all kinds of people, so it's no surprise that the only person ever to infiltrate the Mongols came in under Red Dog's watch.

There were a lot of people at the time who wouldn't deal with Billy, wouldn't talk to him, because they thought he was a cop. There were Mongols who called him a cop to his face. They said so to Junior, but he didn't do anything about it. Even Red Dog was suspicious of him—Queen says that Red Dog put a gun to his head and asked him how long he had been in the police academy. He's the only guy in the history of the Mongols, as far as I know, who was actually accused of being a cop. So maybe he wasn't all that believable.

He accuses us of all kinds of evildoing in his book—gang rape, murder, beating people up for no reason, theft, witness intimidation, and not buying birthday presents for our children. I acknowledge that a lot of that happened before I got in the club, but it doesn't happen anymore, and it's not anything that the Mongols motorcycle club condones or allows, much less plans and organizes. However, many of the things he wrote are either not true or are blown out of all proportion. When I object to these kinds of statements, law enforcement says that we're just trying to cover up our brutality, but that's because they need us to be villains.

He wrote that when he was allowed to see the lists of the membership and the officers of the various chapters that it was clear evidence that the Mongols are a form of organized crime that can be prosecuted under the racketeering laws. If membership lists make us a criminal organization, then I guess he should be infiltrating the Republican and Democratic parties.

He wrote that he saw our record of dues paid and that the dues were acquired through gun trafficking, drug dealing, and extortion. How does he know that the Georgia chapter's dues came from extortion? I can assure you that we don't have any idea where the money comes from.

He wrote that if we throw out a member, we would burn the Mongol tattoo off him. That's ridiculous. I used to hear rumors of such things, but I've never seen it or talked to anyone it happened to. All the clubs used to ask a dismissed member to remove a tattoo, but that meant going to a tattoo shop and covering it up. These stories grow over time and take on a life of their own.

Whenever Billy Queen is asked on television how he could be in the club for two and a half years and never witness a crime taking place (other than people's using drugs), he always said he was lucky. It became a joke with us —here he was in "the most violent motorcycle gang in America" for two years, and he never witnessed a murder, or a rape, or anything like that. We always say that Billy Queen must be the luckiest man in the world.

I wouldn't be surprised if Red Dog and those guys just invented stories to see if Billy would crack. These guys liked to talk and they liked to push it. There are several places in the book where he says he heard the Mongols talk about doing something and he got all scared that he would be involved in a crime. But then nothing ever happened. How can that happen time after time? Well, it could be because we have some members who like to blow some smoke in people's eyes just for the fun of it.

He talked about being at a Ventura run when a cop pulled into the parking lot of the campground and two Mongols talked about killing him. I don't know whether the conversation took place or not, but you would have to be a bonehead to stand there in the middle of a campground and talk about racking a cop. It just wouldn't happen. If you're nutty enough to do it, you're the kind of guy who will sit there quietly and decide to yourself that you're going to blast this guy. Queen gives you the idea that someone was scalped, although he wasn't there; all he actually says is that the man's hair is on the San Fernando Valley chapter flag. There's a photograph that's supposedly of hair and scalp, but all you can see is a ponytail. He says that the flag is in the custody of the ATF, so you kind of wonder why he didn't get a better picture. But I agree those guys in that chapter were bullies and boneheads. They really were capable of anything.

The only Mongol I know of who ever ordered a hit, who told another Mongol to kill someone, was Billy Queen. He writes about it in his book. He's in a bar in the San Fernando Valley, wearing his patch, with four or five other Mongols he believes are carrying guns. They're shooting pool, and some guy comes in and picks a fight. People are always picking fights with us, to prove how tough they are. It's like being the fastest gun in the Old West.

So this guy pulls out a huge bowie knife and makes a sweep across Billy's chest and misses. Billy screams to Rocky, "Shoot him!" He's under attack and there are Mongols there. He wants them to kill this guy with the knife. These bloodthirsty Mongols are watching a member being threatened, which is one of the things we will not allow. What do the Mongols do? Do they kill him? No, they grab the guy, take the knife away from him, sock him a few times until he's not a threat anymore, and throw him out. If we kill at the drop of a hat, why didn't we kill that guy attacking a Mongol?

Suppose the roles had been reversed. Suppose it was a bar full of police officers and a Mongol attacked one of them. Don't you think they would put so many holes in the brother that he would be dead five times over? Not so long ago, there was a homeless woman with a shopping cart downtown. There was an altercation with the police, and the woman pulled out a screwdriver. The police filled her full of lead.

The thing is, this was everyday stuff to us. We deal with violence every day. No matter what Billy thought, that was not an emergency.

Billy Queen did see Mongols beating up people who bothered

them, and he saw people doing drugs. That kind of beating was the first thing I stopped. And I'm not surprised he saw people doing drugs, since every time I met him he asked me if I could get him some drugs. I remember on one of our big runs to the Laughlin casinos, Billy showed up, and I met him in the lobby of our hotel. He asked again—one of many, many times—"Doc, do you know where I can get some dope?" I said I didn't know where to get dope. Then he asked me, "Could you find some if you wanted to?"

Finally I was tired of this and I just wanted to party. "Billy, look," I said, "I could probably find drugs if I wanted to, but that's not what I do. That's not my business. I don't do it for business or for pleasure. That's just not what I do." This is another way the club has changed, because I've made sure that the Mongols are not in the drug business. I know that some of our members do drugs. They don't do them when they're doing Mongol business. How many people in America have done drugs during their lives? I don't use drugs, I don't buy them, I don't sell them, and I don't look for them for anybody. I frown on using drugs, so for me to go and help a brother locate them doesn't make sense.

Queen says we are gun-crazy, but we don't allow guns into our meetings or our club parties. Like I said, I love guns and I collect them. A lot of us do. Chuck Norris does. Steven Spielberg does. A former Texas senator, Phil Gramm, once said he has more shotguns than he needs, but not as many as he wants.

The club has changed since Queen spent time with the San Fernando Valley chapter. He's says at an official Mongol meeting he was told to carry drugs for the club. The club rule in fact is that carrying or holding drugs at a meeting is not allowed. You can't force another member to commit a crime, ever. Now I'm not saying that these things didn't happen with the San Fernando Valley chapter, but if they were doing it, they were breaking club rules. He says that Evel

was the head of a massive, million-dollar stolen-vehicle ring that op-
erated in California and the Southwest. Where did all that money
go? Why are we all poor? I remember some bikes being stolen in
San Fernando one time, and we were all over those guys. I remember telling them, "If you do stupid things, you run a risk of getting
caught and bringing the police down on the whole club."

Evel wasn't even convicted of auto theft, but of transporting stolen
motorcycles across state lines. He deserved to do his time, but it
doesn't make us a criminal empire. Very often, Queen makes a statement about what their investigation hoped to prove, but he never
points out that it didn't prove the allegations. He's very proud of his
investigation, but when you look at the list of the convictions at the
back of his book, almost all of them are for either firearms or drugs.
They did convict Panhead on a murder charge. I'm not saying that
didn't happen, but I don't know one way or the other. I hope that it's
a false conviction, but I can't say.

But you should notice two other things. First, one of the convictions was someone with the California Highway Patrol, a dispatcher.
I don't know exactly what the situation was, and all the book says is
that he provided information to the Mongols, but that happens all
the time. The police will often take sides. For some reason or other,
they are out to get the Mongols, so they will give the Hells Angels
information about where we are or what we're doing. The police
are human too, and if they get hurt, they're going to strike back.
When we were at the height of our war with the Mexican mafia,
a very high ranking police officer came to me after another officer
was killed at a Pomona courthouse and said, "Ruben, La eMe killed
one of my buddies. So I don't care what happens to any of them." He
was really telling me that if someone from La eMe was murdered,
the person who did it would probably not be found out, at least not
by his department. He was giving me the green light to go after La

eMe. Of course, we don't put work in for anybody else, especially not law enforcement, but it shows you how law enforcement can act in certain circumstances.

Second, there are a number of people listed who are not Mongols. They are called "Mongol associates" in the book without any specific explanation. That could be someone who says hello to a Mongol on the street. As far as law enforcement is concerned, anyone who has ever spoken to a Mongol could be a Mongol associate.

The truth is that many of those guys who were convicted were not Mongols. The guys who are truly talented at stealing motorcycles are not members of our club. But sooner or later they're going to have a few beers with some Mongols because we live in the same area, we drink at the same bars, and we are all very interested in motorcycles. We ride them and they steal them. The Mongols have a unique situation among the biker clubs. Most of the biker clubs live in areas that are mainly populated by white people. There aren't that many black biker clubs or Asian bikers clubs, although there are some good ones. But the Mongols live right in some of the toughest gang areas in the country. So we're constantly crossing paths with gangbangers and with people who come out of that life. That makes it easy for outsiders to think that we're part of it too.

I'm not denying that some of our members have bought stolen motorcycles, or even stolen a motorcycle, but it's a small percentage of the membership. The problem is that we come to know some of these people who do steal bikes, and when the police catch them and take them to court, they'll say these guys are known associates of the Mongols.

It's very rare that we have a chance to respond fairly to their accusations. The news media thinks that stories about us sell air time and advertising only when they can make us out to be criminals. What would be the advantage to them to report that most Mongols never commit a crime, or that most Mongols have jobs and contribute to their community?

If you consider it from the point of view of law enforcement, the police have a heavy burden when they start one of these operations. It's very expensive to pay the officer, to create a background story for him, to provide him with an apartment, support personnel for protection and surveillance, and so on for more than two years. So after spending hundreds of thousands of dollars on this undercover operation, they can't simply roll it up and say, "Sorry guys, better luck next time." They need to justify all this time and money with arrests and convictions. So naturally they try to bring in everybody for every possible violation.

Let me show you how it goes. They will throw a raid and pick up every motorcycle that they find on everyone's property. They even go to motorcycle shops, even though the owners aren't Mongols, because they accuse them of being associated with us. They take every motorcycle in the shop, no matter who it belongs to, legal or illegal, and impound them. Then they line up forty motorcycles and have a press conference, and they say we picked up stolen motorcycles in a raid on the Mongols and Mongol associates. In the background on the television news, you see forty motorcycles, so the average taxpayer sees this and says to himself, Whoa! Those Mongols are really bad characters. But what they don't tell you is out of those forty motorcycles, maybe one or two are stolen. And those stolen ones may belong to a Mongol or they may not.

Same with guns. If they break into our houses with a search warrant that allows them to take everything out of the house, they will take all the guns. They line up all those guns on a table along with the patches and everything else and call in the television news to announce that they confiscated weapons. They don't tell you that most of those weapons will come back to the owners down the road because they're all legal. Maybe not all of them, but most of them. So the taxpayers are left with the idea that the police just took fifty, sixty weapons off the streets, but actually they haven't done that at all.

Law enforcement people complain that we don't respect them. It's funny. I've spent my whole life demanding respect, and for the most part, I've gained respect among the people in my life—whether it was in the gang, locked up, or at the hospital. I know about gaining respect. I believe that you have to earn respect, and that's the problem. We see the police up close, not the way most people see them. It's hard to respect them when you see what some of them are doing, and hiding, behind those badges.

I think what they really mean, and what they really don't like, is that we don't fear them. And we don't. When you think about it, why should anybody fear the police? Do we live in a police state, where the police have power beyond the laws? Unfortunately, the Mongols and others like us do live in a police state. We are constantly stopped and searched by the police. They curse us, tell us we're scum and that we shouldn't exist. Even Billy Queen found that out. When that kind of thing happened to me when I was a gangbanger, I expected it. I expected the police to stop me and search me; that was part of the game. But now that I'm living a productive life and contributing to society in a way that is really helpful, I don't see why I should be constantly harassed just because I wear a leather vest with a Mongols patch on it.

I've helped save more lives in my line of work than most of them have saved in theirs. I don't see why the police should curse at me. I don't see why my front door should be rammed in when I've committed no crimes. I don't see why my papers and my personal items—like my Mongol patches—should be confiscated for an indefinite period, sometimes forever. I'm no longer able to keep certain things at my home because I know that the police will eventually swoop in and take it all. I used to keep a file of newspaper clippings of police who had been arrested for worse crimes than the ones we're accused of—like child pornography and other kinds of perversions. But whenever my house is raided, they take all that and never return it to me.

Now I'm not talking about all police officers or all law enforcement officials. There are some good cops. They are the ones who do their job professionally and without preconceived ideas of who we are. I have been arrested in a very professional way. There's a big difference between making a professional arrest and shoving people against a car, yelling at them, kicking them. That's being a thug and a bully. A bully is a bully whether he's a biker or a cop.

All my life, I have disliked and fought against bullies. Unfortunately, there are many members of law enforcement who are no better than bullies and some who are much worse. The bullies are the ones who hide behind their uniform and use it to intimidate people. For instance, we know a lot of the women who work in the strip clubs. For some reason, strippers are especially attracted to Mongols, so we know them pretty well. They tell us which cops take them in and threaten them with jail unless they give the cops sex.

I know of a woman who was a battered wife for many years. She would always say that she fell down the stairs or something like that, but I knew she was being beaten by her husband. Finally, after years of this, she worked up the nerve to call the police and take action against her husband. A police officer came to take her statement, and while she was telling him the story, he started feeling her breasts. Can you imagine that? Can you imagine how she felt when she finally tried to get out from a terrible situation and the person who was supposed to help her started abusing her? How can I respect someone like that?

That's the problem between Mongols and the police. We don't like authority to begin with, and then we see how often these so-called authority figures are just dirty. We know about the law enforcement officers who are either taxing the drug dealers in the neighborhood or doing something else that's either illegal or immoral. And sometimes unnatural. There are cops who take money from the people whose houses they raid. They report half of what they take and they keep the rest. There are police who keep half the *drugs* they seize.

There are deputies in the county system who get trapped by their own weaknesses. They arrest a guy who deals drugs or has power in the streets some other way. This guy might provide the deputy with drugs or with two or three young girls who are willing to do anything for him when he's off duty. This deputy might not get to be with many women, or maybe he needs money. Obviously this deputy is going to reciprocate. The dealer says he has a problem that the deputy could help with—say he needs to get to somebody in jail. The deputy fixes it up and all of a sudden he's basically a criminal. He can't go back and he can't get out. I know that this happens.

But the thing about it is that only we will ever see it. We can see it and survive because they know that we aren't going to testify on anybody, not even on the bad cops. It's just like jail. The system works that way and they know that they're protected. They know that we know but that we're not going to go and say, "This cop is dirty." We see it all, but the public doesn't, and the public wouldn't believe us if we said anything.

Anyway, we know which cops are involved in the drug trade and which ones are extorting money from people and which ones are junkies. So when they stop Mongols, we know that maybe two out of the six cops shaking us down are thugs. Their fellow officers don't know, but we do. And we don't feel like we have to show respect to the thugs. The other officers see this and figure that we're just criminals because we have no respect for the thug cops we know about.

nother interesting thing is that there are some real similarities between some cops and some bikers. One is that they like motorcycles. This just fascinates me: I've had cops stop me and say that if they weren't wearing a police uniform, they would be wearing a Mongol patch. You have law enforcement people who are dying to be the bad boy—like Billy Queen but worse. Those guys have created their own motorcycle clubs made up exclusively of law enforcement people: the Quarry Boys, the Lords of Loyalty, the Wild Pigs, and numerous others. When they're off duty they put on the outfit—the jeans, the bandanna pulled real low over their forehead, they tattoo themselves all up, and they really feel like they're bad boys. They're basically imitating us in every way except one: They're not willing to pay the price that we pay. They're not willing to put up with harassment and the challenges that we live with.

The problem is when they step over to our life, like for instance wearing the California rocker. They figure that because they are the law, even when they're not in uniform, nobody is going to challenge them about it. Well here's the deal—if you're running around dressing and acting like an outlaw biker, going to our bars and everything else, then you have to play by our rules. We don't give a shit what you do when you go to work. This is one of the reasons there are many problems between us and law enforcement. It has nothing to do with us breaking the law. It's really about them dressing up like outlaws and getting in our faces when they're not brave enough to do it without that badge in their pocket. It's a kind of disrespect.

I don't have a problem with somebody who wears a suit and drives a motorcycle back and forth to work. I don't have a problem with some yuppies riding around with their girlfriends for a weekend trip. I know they're nothing like me. And they know it too.

But the cops want to have it both ways. I've been approached by officers riding in their black-and-white patrol car while on duty.

They stop me and say, "You guys control the streets while you're out there on your bikes, but we control them while we're in our black-and-whites. We can make your lives miserable." That is somebody getting paid by our taxes, but he's confronting me just like a gang member would. He's not saying anything about me breaking the law. He's just talking about control.

I remember once going to Palm Springs on a bike run. About three hundred of us were going to roll into Palm Springs to party, but I showed up with ten members before the pack got there. I had heard that the Lords of Loyalty, a club that is mostly CHP, were downtown, all dressed up with their bandannas on their heads and everything, and they were flying the California rocker. So I found them at a sidewalk café, and they were all sitting looking at us hard, like they were some hard-core club. They made some remarks about us, and we made some back. This is not a cop in his patrol car, remember; these are just some individuals from another motorcycle club.

Luckily when the Palm Springs police found out that the Mongols were rolling in down the highway, they immediately rushed to these biker cops and told them they'd better get the hell out of there: "There are three hundred Mongols coming in here, and we're not ready for a confrontation between you guys." The Palm Springs police actually escorted them out of town—one group of cops escorted another group of cops out of town.

They say we don't respect cops, but we do—at least the cops who deserve it. I think every man no matter what should be respected; when you first meet the man, you should give him the respect that you would want. And then when you find out what he's all about, you'll see what respect he's earned. Some maybe don't deserve it, but at least to begin with, it doesn't matter what he looks like, what he's into, you need to go ahead and treat him with respect. He's a man.

But there are these cops who want to be heroes. They live in a fantasy world where they are the knight in shining armor. And in order to be the knight they need to have villains. From movies like *The Wild One,* they get the idea that bikers ride into town and rape everybody. They actually transfer that to life on the streets. Billy Queen writes it in his book and says it when he's doing publicity events. Unfortunately, even he knows that it's not true. I have Billy Queen on tape in a courtroom being asked about the Mongols committing rape. I finally got tired of hearing him say that the Mongols were rapists, and I had our lawyer question him about it. The lawyer asked, "Did you ever see the Mongols rape anyone during the time you were a Mongol?" Queen said no. "Have you ever seen or ever heard of the Mongols raping a woman while you were a Mongol?" He said no. "Isn't it true that, as far as you know, rape is nonexistent in the Mongol motorcycle club?" and he said, "That is correct." All under oath.

If you're going to talk like a thug and act like a thug, then we're going to treat you like a thug, whether you're in uniform or not. One time at a bar in West Covina called National Sports Grill, five of us were having some drinks, and we were wearing our colors. We were having a good time when a guy comes over and starts mouthing off and calling us assholes and saying more or less somebody ought to teach us a lesson. I said, "Fuck off. Who do you think you are?"

He pulled out his wallet and flipped it open to show me his badge. And he looked at me like that was the end of it. He's in there drinking and talking a lot of crap, and he figures that as soon as he pulls out that badge everybody will back off.

I grabbed the wallet and threw it as far as I could—over six pool tables, all the way to the end of the room. As it flew across the pool tables, his cards and papers fell out of the wallet and scattered over the floor, and everybody was staring. He looked at me like he couldn't believe what I'd done. Just stood there. He didn't do a damn thing.

I said, "I don't give a fuck who you are during the day. If you're coming here and you're going to start shit with me you're going to deal with it."

Right there I could see his mind start to work. He was thinking, *Wait a minute, I've been drinking, these guys are going to start something, and it's going to end up on a police report.* I turned around and watched him through the mirrors on the bar as he gathered up his papers and left.

I'm sure that down the line he's going to catch one of us while he's in his patrol car. He'll take his revenge then, while he's getting paid by the city, behind the badge. Or, for instance, a few months later, the police will issue a bulletin that says something like "We have received information that the Mongols are going to attempt to kill a police officer." That riles up police in other areas and other departments, and the level of harassment just goes off the charts. That's the only way these guys can even up the score with us, because they're afraid to start a fight with us, to actually get into a physical confrontation. It's a shame, because they'll start something on the street as a biker, but they pick up on it again inside their black-and-whites.

What I think is very strange is that after all these years, Billy Queen is still wearing his Mongol paraphernalia when he goes on television. If we're as despicable as he says—rapists, murders, thieves, wife beaters, and all the rest—why is he still wearing the Mongol hat and gear? I would never wear, say, a Charles Manson T-shirt or a Richard Ramirez cap. I wouldn't be caught dead celebrating a rapist or anyone who kills innocents. They're despicable characters. If we're everything he says we are, why did he become so close to us? Why was he ready to quit the ATF and spend his life riding with the Mongols? His story doesn't add up. The hypocrisy of it disgusts me.

One of the hardest parts of being me, really, is that I have to sit there and listen. People talk about us on television and write about us in the newspaper and the police give their version of events, but I know the true story behind it all and I just have to live with it. I watch this Billy Queen talk, and I think to myself, *What a crock of shit*. Worse is that he says it and the public believes him, and the public gets an image of us. And the image snowballs as others pick up on the idea and the police feed the hunger for violent news. Then the same stories get rehashed and picked over, and everybody's record is pulled out for the world to see. Unfortunately, in trying to create a villain, they ruin people's lives. They create the monster and they add to it, like Billy still does to this day on TV.

We won't change the way we are. But we're not what they say.

13

Life Goes On

few months ago, I was contacted by some Ukrainians, who are very, very serious people. They asked for a meeting, and I agreed, because it's safer. If you say you won't talk to them, they'll find you. I could walk into my home and they would be sitting on my sofa. And people like that respect balls. I have more chance of surviving if I walk into a meeting than if I try to fight off an attack. I always talk to everyone. It just works out better that way.

So I went to the meeting, which was in the basement of a nightclub in Hollywood. The club was closed at the time. They took me downstairs, and it was like a scene out of a movie: a guy sitting at a table with one light swinging overhead and two massive guys standing behind him. He motioned for me to sit down, and he presented me with an offer. He said that they were in the business of transporting women from Eastern Europe and Ukraine and that area to the United States through Canada. They were called maids or something like that, but it was pretty clear that he was basically in the business of sexual slavery. He asked me if the Mongols would like to be paid to provide security for this. He said he could pay very well.

"I don't think I can do that," I said. It wasn't that we don't provide people for security, and of course Little Rubes is a professional at it. "I consider that profiting from human misery. I really can't ask my people to work for something that I don't think is acceptable." I was basically telling him to fuck off, but I didn't hesitate for a second. This was disgusting.

He tried to convince me a little bit more, but I was very definite about it. Finally, he gave up. I turned to leave, wondering if someone would put a bullet in my back. Then I noticed that a bodyguard had appeared at the foot of the stairs. I looked at him and he looked at me. I kept walking, and as I passed him, he said a few words in his language. I don't speak it, but I could hear the words in my head the whole way home. When you're in that kind of situation, you're very alert. You notice every detail.

I got into contact with someone who spoke Ukrainian and asked him to translate for me. After I repeated the words, he said, "Respect few, fear none."

I guess our reputation has traveled a long way.

Another time, I got a message from someone on the East Coast who is a member of a very dangerous club. He was asking about this guy named Jesse James, who has become a bit famous on the West Coast for building beautiful custom motorcycles. He builds for all of the clubs, but at a motorcycle show on the East Coast, he was showing some bikes he had built for Hells Angels. The message was: "We're going to buy up all his products. Is that cool?"

I knew that this was a death sentence for Jesse, and very serious. To make sure about Jesse, I called up Emilio "Chino" Gonzalez, a friend of mine who builds custom cars. He had done a television show with Jesse. I told him the situation. "Doc, this guy's just a businessman. He works for everybody, even Mongols." So my response to the East Coast club member was "That's a negative. Jesse James is OK." In the end, for whatever reason, nothing happened. Jesse later gave me an excellent small statue of a Genghis Khan Mongol. I was happy to help.

But the life goes on. In the summer of 2007, I got a call one night. It was my brother, Al. "I've been shot," he said.

"Who did it?" I didn't need to tell him that I was worried about him and that I would take care of him. But if he was going to die, I wanted to know who did it. He didn't know, but we'll find out.

He was driving on the freeway when a car pulled up next to him and fired a burst into his SUV. One bullet shattered the bone in his left arm and lodged in his chest, but he was still able to get off the freeway and make it to a gas station. There was a line of bullet holes in the post between the front door and the back door. If their aim had been just a bit better, Al would not have survived.

When I got down to the gas station, it was a complete mess. The police had roped off the area and were throwing all the trash out of the Dumpsters. Naturally, they suspected the Mongols had started it. Thinking that Al had fired the first shot, they were going through the trash to see if he'd thrown away a weapon.

Al has recovered, but we'll have to take care of this. One of the things we always say is, "Don't poke a sleeping bear with a stick." Once the bear is roused, he's much more dangerous than your stick.

oday I live in West Covina, to the east of Los Angeles. It's quiet, there are trees, I can sit outside, I don't hear gunshots every minute, and there are no helicopters with spotlights hovering over me. Except when the police decide to raid me.

Not long ago, I had a wedding in my backyard. It was a family wedding, which is really the only kind of socializing I do anymore outside of the Mongols, except for an occasional barbecue someone at work might throw where it's easier for me to go than not to. Everyone at work knows I'm the head of the Mongols. My supervisors came to the clubhouse, but some of my coworkers would rather not talk about the Mongols, which is fine with me. I prefer it that way. Some civilians are afraid of me. It's not something I strive for, but I guess it goes with the territory.

Because the law knows I now live in West Covina, they park a car on the hillside across the way and constantly watch the front of my house. Each time a car leaves, the surveillance team radios ahead and a waiting patrol car pulls it over. They search the passengers and everything inside the car.

Everybody who left the wedding that day was subjected to the routine. It wasn't even a Mongol function, just a family wedding, but it didn't make any difference. That's what they keep doing, and as far as I'm concerned it's totally illegal. It's not illegal to be a Mongol, it's not illegal to visit a Mongol. They found nothing.

When I walk into a bar or a restaurant or a stadium and I have my paraphernalia on and people look, that feeling is one of pride. People are very interested in the Mongols, and a lot of them admire us. I know that they know I'm somebody. They may think somebody crazy or somebody special, but somebody. Somebody who doesn't get pushed around.

We may have our problems within the club, but there's no equal to being a Mongol. All I want to do right now is to keep the club growing and expanding. We now have more than two thousand members, and chapters all over the country and in Canada and Italy. Every month we attract dozens of new members. The more popular we get, the more people want to join us. I guess there's always a danger that we'll become too popular and maybe even too close to being a part of the mainstream, which would go against everything we believe in. We've talked about it among ourselves and are extremely careful to keep that from ever happening. I guess it's one of the hazards of popularity and admiration.

People always want to take their pictures with us. They come up all timid and ask if it would be all right, and most of the time we say yes. It's a form of wearing the colors, isn't it? People love to fantasize about wearing our colors. When people see us going down the highway, they look at us with admiration. Even if they don't like us, they know we've earned the right to be Mongols. That means something, to them and to us.

BRONSON: IN MEMORIAM

In a Small Nevada Gambling Town

On the banks of the Colorado River,
As the river boats paddled and the dice did their dance,
While the town bristled with players of chance,
The deafening roar preceded the posse, the sound very near.
Women and daughters were hurried along, most out of fear.
From each corner of town men yelled,
"The Mongols are here!"
Those who trailered their bikes and
Pretended to be strong
Took cover and shook in their chaps and their thongs.
They would later complain "It's too scary for us."
They would plead to the law to hurry and solve
And jail both of those clubs who were truly involved.
As the Mongols rode in they were met by the law.
They were asked to turn in any weapons at all.
The law said it's our town and we will handle it all.
The Mongols were forbidden from town and that hotel that is pink;
They were also tired of being challenged, I think.
They'd nothing to prove and sat down for a drink
At Rosa's Cantina, their watering hole.
Though they were unarmed and forbidden from town
The Mongols went on without even a frown.
With their loved ones in town, and half in their slumber
They noticed them coming all neat in a row
With their six shooters, bowies, and even some lumber.

While Johnny Law watched, wives they did scatter
And slot machine chatter gave way to the sound
Of six-shooters blazing as men hit the ground.
The air ran foul with gun smoke and feathers
And though several men died there was one unlike others.
He lives in the hearts of all his true brothers.
Now, very few get to prove they can live as a Mongol;
Fewer still get to prove they can die as one too.
To those who brag and say they're worldwide,
If you could ask those you buried after they died,
They would tell you those Mongols can fight with pure pride.
Like the OK Corral, it is history now.
Like the days of Ike Clayton, the Earps, and Jameses,
Those days of Zapata and Villa are gone.
Things haven't changed much in this old Wild West
Where the fastest gun, *still,* is put to the test.

    Bronson,
    Thinking of you, Bro,
    Doc

    (*Although I am not a poet, after Laughlin, this came out from someplace I didn't know I had.*)

EPILOGUE

was the international president of the Mongols Motorcycle Club up until the end of 2008 when authorities arrested approximately sixty Mongols in a sting operation. The arrests were a result of a three-year investigation by federal agents posing as fellow M.C. members. I'm being held, without bail, awaiting trial for charges of racketeering.

CHAPTER 13

Out on the West Coast where it all began,
Down in California, some call the promised land,
Live the Mongols M.C. They stand a head above the rest.
Yeah, we've met the challenge and passed the test.

Now at the heart of those Brothers who stand a head above the rest
Lives Chapter 13, the best of the best.
The chapter was established back in '74
When a Brother named Melo opened the door.

Up in Delano one hot summer night
Ol' mellow Melo got into a fight.
He beat in some faces and kicked some ass,
Then sat down at the bar to finish his glass.

When it was time to call it a night,
Ol' Brother Melo went out to his bike.
But the cowardly punks he'd whipped in the bar
Were lying in wait outside by their car.

They shot and they shot through their sights
And then they ran off like rats in the night.
Our Brother lay dead. He chartered Chapter 13,
The best of the best of Mongols M.C.

Now over the years, the chapter has grown.
The numbers add up. Ol' Melo's not alone.
The reason for this is known far and wide:
We never back down. We live Mongol pride.

So if you should go there and meet my old Bros,
Better watch what you say, don't step on no toes.
You're in Mongol country and it's real plain to see,
We're Mongols forever—forever Mongols M.C.

—Poor Boy

THE FALLEN BROTHERS

Melo	Aug. 15th, 1974
McCloud	Aug. 3rd, 1976
Turtle	Oct. 17th, 1976
Plowboy	Jul. 29th, 1977
Red Beard	Sept. 5th, 1977
Jingles	Sept. 5th, 1977
Welo	Nov. 26th, 1977
LiL Frank	Jul. 30th, 1978
R.J.	Mar. 9th, 1981
Heavy	Apr. 18th, 1981
Red	Jun. 28th, 1981
Ronnie	Oct. 5th, 1981
Buzz	Jun. 10th, 1982
G.P.	Jun. 10th, 1982
Sleepy	Jul. 18th, 1982
Bull Dog	Apr. 2nd, 1983
Rick	Apr. 23rd, 1983
Stitches	May 20th, 1984
O'Henry	May 20th, 1984
Half-breed	Jan. 25th, 1985
Catfish	Jul. 4th, 1988
Cowboy	Feb. 14th, 1991
Papa Tony	Sept. 15th, 1992
Loose Bruce	Oct. 16th, 1995

Slo Joe	Mar. 17th, 1998
Shoe String	May 22nd, 1998
Cowboy	Oct. 10th, 1988
Marvin	Oct. 21st, 1988
Skin	Feb. 14th, 1999
Conan	Nov. 22nd, 2001
Pirate	Apr. 14th, 2002
Bronson	Apr. 27th, 2002
Popcorn	Oct. 4th, 2002
Bishop	Nov. 14th, 2002
Pervert	Feb. 24th, 2003
Ghost	Apr. 1st, 2003
Caballo	May 11th, 2003
Spider	Aug. 3rd, 2003
Crook	Dec. 7th, 2003
P.K.	Jan. 10th, 2004
Double-D	Mar. 18th, 2004
Lil Benny	Sept. 7th, 2004
John-T	Oct. 22nd, 2004
Shark	Mar. 6th, 2005
Chip	Apr. 22nd, 2005
Sonic	Nov. 5th, 2005
Crazy Andy	Jan. 11th, 2006
Boy	Sept. 3rd, 2006
Tudy	Nov. 6th, 2006
Oso	May 25th, 2007
Smokes	Oct. 20th, 2007

ACKNOWLEDGMENTS

I would like to thank everyone who helped to make this book a reality, especially my friend and agent Alan Nevins of the Firm Entertainment, who saw the value of this project when it was still a diamond in the rough, and his colleagues Mindy Stone and Anthony Mattero; Walter Bode, whose professionalism made writing the book seem easy; and my editor, Mauro DiPreta, who stayed with it even when the going got tough, and his colleague Jennifer Schulkind.